CONTENTS

	Acknowledgements	iv
SECTION 1	Introduction: a framework for playful teaching	1
SECTION 2	The practitioner-researchers: who are we and what do we do?	13
SECTION 3	Using the materials within the Pack: let the children – and practitioners – play!	19
SECTION 4	Using the video: what we can learn by observing children and practitioners playing	23
SECTION 5	The Statements of Entitlement to Play: explanation and charts	37
SECTION 6	StEPs and curricular links	57
SECTION 7	Using the six entitlements: interpreting StEPs in action in the setting	73
SECTION 8	Child development charts	89
	References	95
	Annotated bibliography: early years texts	99
	Topic index	105
	Author index	107

ACKNOWLEDGEMENTS

The research project that underpins this Pack has had the involvement of so many that however long our list of acknowledgements someone will surely be left out. Suffice it to say, that in terms of the settings, staff, children and parents, we are indebted to them all for working with us on the process of examining play practices.

Jon and Carl from the Audio Visual Unit at University of Leicester also found themselves engaged in a playful process with a lot of hard work attached to it. Without them and their good humour in filming, re-filming, cutting, editing, refining and sifting through the wealth of settings-based material, the Pack would be incomplete. We owe them (and Siân Adams, who acted as liaison and editor for the video) a real debt of gratitude for an excellent outcome to their energies.

The Esmée Fairbairn Charitable Trust are also acknowledged for their financial support of the project over 2 years, its funding providing the necessary time for practitioners to meet, discuss, argue, challenge and generally reflect on the processes of teaching and learning through play. Alongside this, the University of Leicester provided other financial and academic support for which we were all extremely grateful.

We inevitably also give thanks to each other for facilitating the process of reflecting on practices that challenged – and continue to challenge – all of us as we strive to make education and learning more meaningful for children and more enjoyable and playful for adults.

Janet Moyles and colleagues

StEPs: STATEMENTS OF ENTITLEMENT TO PLAY
A framework for playful teaching with 3–7-year-olds

Janet Moyles and Siân Adams
with
Jill Evans, Helen Geisler, Sue Gray, Liz Magraw, Pat Medland, Claire Orton, Debbie Pentecost, Vivien Robins, Gillian Simpson

Open University Press
Buckingham • Philadelphia

Open University Press
22 Ballmoor
Buckingham
MK18 1XW

email: enquiries@openup.co.uk
world wide web: www.openup.co.uk

and
325 Chestnut Street
Philadelphia, PA 19106, USA

First Published 2001
Reprinted 2002

Copyright © Janet Moyles and Siân Adams, 2001

All rights reserved. Except for the quotation of short passages for the purpose of criticism and review, no part of this publication may be reproduced, stored in a retrieval system, or transmitted, in any form or by any means, electronic, mechanical, photocopying, recording or otherwise, without the prior written permission of the publisher or a licence from the Copyright Licensing Agency Limited. Details of such licences (for reprographic reproduction) may be obtained from the Copyright Licensing Agency Ltd of 90 Tottenham Court Road, London, W1P 0LP.

A catalogue record of this book is available from the British Library

ISBN 0 335 20717 0

Library of Congress Cataloging-in-Publication Data
Moyles, Janet R.
   StEPs: statements of entitlement to play : a framework for playful teaching / Janet Moyles and Siân Adams with Jill Evans . . . [et al.].
       p. cm.
   Includes bibliographical references and index.
   ISBN 0-335-20717-0
   1. Play. 2. Early childhood education.
   I. Adams, Siân, 1946– II. Title.

LB1140.35.P55 M69 2001
372.21–dc21   00-068922

Typeset in 10/13pt Meridien by Graphicraft Limited, Hong Kong
Printed and bound in Great Britain by
Marston Book Services Limited, Oxford

SECTION ONE

Introduction: a framework for playful teaching

This Pack contains a comprehensive set of Statements of Entitlement to Play (StEPs), supported by a video and other materials, which have been developed by a group of early years practitioners for use in a range of settings providing for the education and development of children up to the age of 7 years. The age span deliberately encompasses the very early years, the Foundation Stage and Key Stage One of the National Curriculum, for the writers of the Pack believe strongly that these years are crucial to all attempts to develop a lifelong learning society. This is *the* crucial period in children's lives when, above all else, their development will – and must – determine the learning opportunities provided. This includes learning about oneself and one's own capabilities, which, in turn, determine what young children will believe about themselves as learners and how the rest of society views them as learners. If society believes they have rights and responsibilities, this is what children themselves will grow up to believe. If, however, society views them as incompetent, without political and cultural awareness and a general drain on resources, then that is potentially what they will become.

THE PACK'S VALUES

The basis of this pack is a belief in the rights of children to appropriate opportunities to **be** children and to learn in playful and meaningful ways. It is also predicated upon a view that practitioners working with young children have equal rights to teach using appropriate playful strategies with children's entitlement to play uppermost in their minds.

Children and adults are responsible for making the most of the playful learning and teaching opportunities provided in quality early childhood settings and to ensure that the curriculum – statutory or recommended – is implemented efficiently and effectively. We believe strongly that there is **no** conflict between being accountable to parents, politicians or providers for children's learning and offering play experiences as the basis for that learning. The difficulty, we have discovered, rests in the ability of practitioners to substantiate their firm beliefs and values in the strengths of a curriculum based on play, with actual articulation to others of the reasons why play is so crucial to children's development and learning (see Adams 2000; Adams & Moyles 2000).

THE MATERIALS WITHIN THE PACK

Playful teaching and learning are discussed and exemplified throughout the Pack. They are also shown in the accompanying video (see Section 4), which offers viewers a chance to see some of the practitioners in their own settings using aspects of StEPs to support their everyday teaching and learning. One of the main aims of the Pack is that it should be used by practitioners and settings – or those undertaking training sessions with them – both to evaluate and extend play practices. The video, child development charts, planning sheets and other documentation, explained in various sections, support a variety of uses across a range of settings reflecting different backgrounds and ethos. Once the framework is understood, the StEPs themselves offer endless opportunities for development of quality learning experiences for children and for articulation, explanation and advocacy of quality practice by practitioners to parents, inspectors and those who externally evaluate settings.

The video is deliberately short and concise because we feel it is more worthwhile and useful to see just a few minutes of video several times rather than watching endless hours of someone else's practice. Each section of the video represents one or more of the Entitlements and each scene is taken from a longer scenario that shows **actual** classroom practice being undertaken by **real** practitioners. The accompanying planning sheets show the practitioners' intentions and how these link with the StEPs and with child development information.

Similar cameo 'stories' are told in different parts of the Pack so that readers can themselves empathize and engage with the experiences and events in the everyday settings on which the Pack is based and from which it draws its inspiration and exemplars. We feel strongly that the use of such visual imagery is important for readers in considering their own settings and practice, offering the possibility to get 'inside' other settings and review the learning needs of other children without leaving your seat!

Figure 1.1 shows how the various parts of the Pack fit into the overall framework we have evolved

INTRODUCTION: A FRAMEWORK FOR PLAYFUL TEACHING

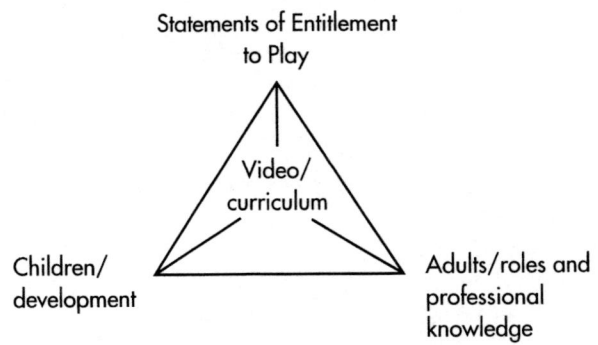

Figure 1.1 A model to explain the framework underpinning StEPs

(how will be explained a little later). For the rest of this Introduction, we will indicate a little of the background to how the Pack came to be formulated and give further details on its values base.

IT ALL STARTED WITH...

Picture the scene... a supervising tutor is visiting a student on placement in a nursery. Children, being as they are, approach the tutor curiously, asking her what she is doing. When she tells them that she has come to see them working, the children laugh and tell her 'We're playing!' and proceed to outline a range of activities they have played during the morning. Eventually, the visiting adult asks, 'Do the grown-ups play with you?' The children are horrified! 'Oh, no! They're too busy to play!'

This comment was sufficient to set a group of experienced practitioners and early years researchers – all qualified nursery nurses and teachers – wondering about their role in children's play. Are we just providers of resources? Do we merely plan for children to be involved in play? How and should we engage ourselves in play?

Having bought this Pack, you have no doubt been asking yourself some of these same questions. As people concerned with young children's education and learning, we all ask many such questions about play and learning; including quite apparently basic ones such as:

- What is play?
- Do children really learn through play?
- What is the adult's role?
- Do others value play in the same way?
- What kind of provision should I make for play?

- Can I afford the time to play?
- How can I justify play when there is so much to fit in?

These are just some of the questions which the group came together to explore 3 years ago. The opportunity arose because of funding obtained from a charitable foundation[1] which supported, for six terms, an on-going process of discussion, questioning, challenge, analysis of practice, introspection and some pain! (It is interesting to note that, despite such pain, the group continued to meet on a regular basis in their own time when the supply cover funding had run out.) Through our meetings and various communications, we attempted to resolve some of the issues that arose from our many questions about adults' roles in children's play and learning and the value of play.

EXPLORING OUR BELIEFS AND VALUES

In developing this Pack as part of our practitioner-based research, our aim is to share with you the results of the very challenging process in which the eleven of us have been engaged and which we know will be of equal concern and interest to similar groups of early childhood educators. For example, early evaluations of our own thinking and practice revealed that, while we declared our whole-hearted commitment to the value of play, there was little clarity or substance in our understanding of the role of the practitioner in planning for, assessing and developing children's learning in this way. At one point, the issue was raised of 'Why do we provide home area play?'; this apparently straightforward question left experienced practitioners floundering when it came to detailing the rationale for this type of provision in relation to children's all-round learning and development. Although it was easy to discuss provision in resource terms, it was much more difficult to delve more deeply into underlying learning and development issues. It is salutary to try to respond to some of the seemingly simple questions that underpin our everyday practice but which are not necessarily articulated regularly. For example:

- What is the child standing at the water tray actually doing and learning?

- Do children learn in ways other than through play?
- How do adults and children distinguish between play and work?

The practitioner-researchers (whose backgrounds and interests are outlined in Section 2) come from a range of contexts mainly with an 'education' focus. During the 3 years of the project, the profile of early years education has been raised significantly, although not always to children's advantage! There has indeed been an unprecedented focus on early childhood curricula resulting, for example, in the Early Learning Goals and their exemplifications materials (QCA 2000a,b). What has been evident – and joyful – throughout the development of the Pack, is the unanimity of the group on the vital importance of working with a sound understanding of child development and the deepening of our beliefs and values about playful teaching and learning. The notion of 'playful teaching' became paramount; hence the title of the Pack.

An analysis of the relationship between the practitioners and the children led us to develop a series of principles – those things that we were not prepared to compromise in considering children's play and learning! We realized quite quickly that, having developed over 100 principles, these were overlapping, unwieldy and largely impractical. Even reducing them to less than 20 proved still to be overwhelming and impossible to translate into practice. As examples, we decided that 'Play is practice for life' and 'Play is cultural', but neither of these could be adopted straightforwardly in daily practice. Something else was needed to bridge the rhetoric and reality divide.

By a very evolutionary process of prioritizing (with much debate and argument), we defined six clear Statements of Entitlement to Play (StEPs):

> 1 Young children are entitled to play experiences that engage them affectively and socially in their own and others' learning.
> 2 Young children are entitled to play experiences that are set in meaningful and relevant activities and contexts for learning.
> 3 Young children are entitled to play experiences that promote curiosity and the use of imagination and creativity in learning.
> 4 Young children are entitled to engage in play experiences that are open-ended and offer trial-and-error learning without fear of failure.
> 5 Young children are entitled to playful, exploratory and experiential activities with a variety of materials and resources and within a variety of contexts.
> 6 Young children are entitled to engage in individual and dynamic play and learning experiences relevant to their age group and stage of development.
>
> [The complementary and interdependent nature of the Entitlements must be emphasized, the numbers being used for reference rather than to indicate priority.]

These much more 'human' and specific statements focus essentially on the learner, and enable practitioners to take each statement as an underpinning rationale for making effective provision. One could argue that these Entitlements apply to learners of all ages, including the practitioner-researchers!

WHY THE WORD 'ENTITLEMENT'?

In using the word 'entitlement', we feel we are reasserting the **centrality of children in their education and their right to be involved in the processes of their own learning**. This means that those who work with young children must respect them and honour their right to a developmentally appropriate curriculum. As practitioners we feel privileged to work with young children and their families; this is what keeps most of us motivated and interested in our jobs. Practitioners must be prepared, as we have done, to articulate clearly and with conviction – through a deepening knowledge and understanding of children and providing for their education – the clear and indisputable reasons for working with children from this entitlements-based stance.

For the individuals within the research group, StEPs (and the on-going analysis of their own classroom practices with these in mind) has become the backbone of their practice. Implicit within the Entitlements is the ability to provide for equality of

INTRODUCTION: A FRAMEWORK FOR PLAYFUL TEACHING

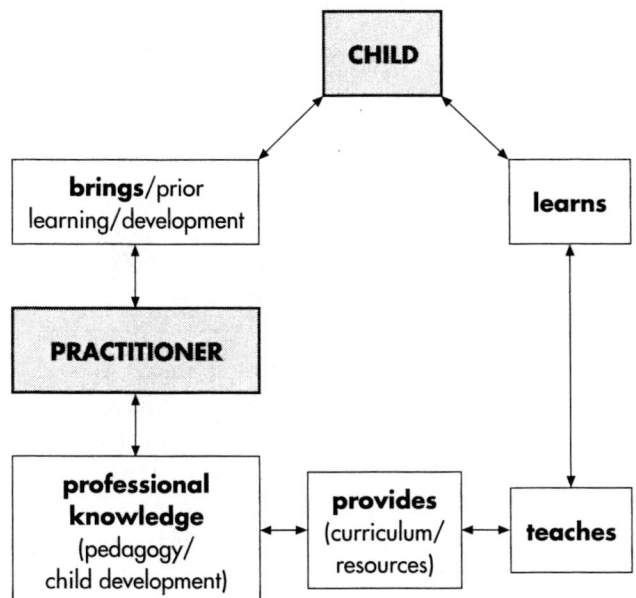

Figure 1.2 A model to explain the framework underpinning StEPs

curricular provision, which are explained both earlier in this Introduction and in subsequent sections. These were epitomized by the group in the above model outlining the overall framework of StEPs and how they operate in practice in settings for children up to the age of 7 years.

Practitioners can begin at any point on this model. For example, the practitioner *provides* sand play opportunities for 4-year-olds. What aspects will the practitioner need to *teach* to ensure that the children *learn*? Which *children* and what aspects of *development* will predominate? What do the children already bring to the situation by way of *prior learning and experiences*? What does the *practitioner* need to think about and what *professional knowledge* is already available to them about sand play and about these particular 4-year-olds. What physical development can be anticipated and will this affect the children in any other aspects of their development?

Another example starting from a different point would be:

opportunity across culture, ethinicity, faith, gender, family background, special educational needs or disability. We have discovered that these entitlement statements offer a systematic approach to planning, assessment and curriculum provision for young children, enabling practitioners themselves to engage in a process of self-evaluation in a non-threatening and flexible way.

FOR WHOM IS StEPs INTENDED?

All of you who, in your everyday lives, need to address the challenge of providing playful teaching and learning for children up to 7 years of age, will want to use StEPs as a basis for planning and evaluation. It is structured so that you can approach planning for learning from a number of complementary angles, which are explained within different sections of the Pack, and in the explanatory model (Figure 1.2).

A MODEL OF EARLY YEARS PEDAGOGY

The Pack is predicated upon certain beliefs and ideologies about children, practitioners and

> A 5-year-old enters the reception class. Information about the *child* and his *prior learning and development* is gathered by talking to the parents and reading records from the previous placement. The child is very interested in picture books and insists on always having one at hand. From the *practitioner's* own *knowledge and experience*, there is a realization that the child understands the full range of strategies, which means he can easily become a reader. The child is clearly 'ready' for the next stage and should be *provided* with books that have meaningful print. However, so as not to affect the child's confidence as a beginning reader, the practitioner will need to *teach* by reading the words alongside the child and encouraging the parents to do so as well. Therefore, the practitioner will need to work with parents in understanding the level at which their child is currently *learning*. What the child then *learns* will build on his current developmental level in terms of emotional, linguistic and cognitive aspects.

Yet another example would be for the practitioner to start from the level of resources:

> One practitioner-researcher was concerned that the resources *provided* for numeracy in the setting appeared rather narrow because children's *prior knowledge* of maths from the home circumstances was limited – and, to a certain extent, limiting – as was the organization of resources in the setting. She based this judgement on her developing *professional knowledge* that *children* did not have access to the resources for a sufficient time that they were able to gain *confidence, competence* and *independence* or *learn* to appreciate mathematics as a tool for learning. By *teaching* children how to develop their abilities to make repeating patterns, to sort, match and count, the practitioner ensured that the children were able to show their learning and to reinforce it.

It is possible to see that the model offers the opportunity for a wide range of planning, assessment and self-evaluation activities. As examples, when considering the sand play example above:

- What range of resources is readily available and what might need to be purchased?
- Do the practitioners understand what it is they need to teach and, if not, what in-service activities would be useful?
- Would it be useful to consider an audit of professional knowledge across a particular setting so that the skills and understandings of all can be utilized effectively (see Moyles and Suschitzky 1998a,b)?
- Does the setting have sufficient recorded information to know what the child has already achieved and what prior learning and experiences have been accomplished?

WHERE DOES THE CURRICULUM FIT IN WITH StEPs?

The Curriculum is everything that affects the child in the learning environment, overt and covert. It covers not only the activities, both indoors and outdoors, offered to young children, but the attitudes of the staff towards the children and each other, to parents and anyone who visits the setting...

(Curtis 1998: 21)

Given the above definition of curriculum, there is no conflict with StEPs – in fact, quite the reverse! The StEPs charts represent a wider view of curriculum and its implementation, which rests firmly in making provision to meet children's needs.

Look more closely within the columns and statements and it will become apparent quite quickly that the whole curriculum, including subjects, are definitely there, albeit implicitly. There are many examples in the video and other written cameos of literacy, numeracy and other subject learning and exemplification shows how these are incorporated into the StEPs framework. In fact, going back to the model in Figure 1.2, it is possible to see that if we commence on the cycle at 'teaches', then this could equally have a subject as its basis. Another example based on the model in Figure 1.2 might help at this point.

The Literacy Strategy is a requirement for teaching at Key Stage 1 (unless one has good reason not to!).

> The practitioner plans to *teach* the 6-year-old children a short, humorous poem that will be used throughout the week to emphasize particular rhyming words and initial letter names and sounds. She plans that the children will *learn* the necessary content and give evidence of this learning by using the rhyming words in a puppet play that they have been developing. Each *child* has been observed during the previous week in their play by the teacher to see what *existing understanding* of the 'new' rhyming words, compound words and revision of initial letters they possess and the teacher has noted their *prior knowledge*. She has noticed that one child finds particular types of sounds difficult and discovers, in reading around the issues to extend her *professional knowledge*, that this is because of an inability to make appropriate shapes with his mouth and lips (*physical development*). It is also apparent that he acts in a 'silly' way when speaking through the puppets and her *experience* tells her that this is probably to cover up the difficulty he is experiencing. The teacher will *provide* safety mirrors in the home and puppet areas to encourage the child to play with words and sounds so that he can 'see' what mouth shapes he is making and ask the assistant to play sound games with him using the mirror. Part of what she has *provided* is a range of objects for the puppets to talk about, which begin with the focus on initial sounds.

INTRODUCTION: A FRAMEWORK FOR PLAYFUL TEACHING

There are many examples of curriculum provision within the Pack and we feel certain that you will be able to add your own subject labels. But remember that the child – not the subject – should be the focus of your teaching.

BEGIN AT THE BEGINNING...

There is a danger with Packs such as this that they can be thought of as prescriptions for good practice, which, if followed scrupulously, will provide all the answers! While we all, in the busy world of early childhood, feel the need for 'quick fixes', every context and every group of children is different.

We are quite adamant that this is not a 'how-to-do-it' pack

What we have done is to provide a clear framework that allows practitioners to work from a range of different starting points. No one section within the StEPs charts (see Section 5) stands alone. Whether you start from the children and their needs (as we mainly have), from the practitioner's knowledge (as we have increasingly done) or from the point of view of resource provision (which we've tried to move away from!), it is necessary to ensure that all elements of the model are worked towards achieving a cohesive, comprehensive and rounded curriculum for all children.

We have tried to keep sight of all the issues surrounding work with young children that practitioners must address to embrace the wider aspects of curriculum provision and implementation. These include the following, with the capital letters in parentheses indicating the column in the Entitlement Charts in which this aspect is found:

- working from the basis of *children's prior experiences* and knowledge (Column A);
- using different aspects of *child development* to become informed about where children 'are' (Column B);
- considering what *new learning* is necessary and sensible for children (Column C);
- thinking about the *professional and pedagogic knowledge*, experience and understanding of practitioners (Column D);
- examining the management of settings and *resource provision* across the curriculum (Column E);
- what and how it is most appropriate for practitioners to *teach* (Column F).

These are the key aspects that have been used to delineate the 'steps' within each of our StEPs. These headings enable each setting to make clear links between teaching, learning and resources in a way that maximizes them all and makes them coherent; we will show you how this works in later sections. Strengths already exist in many of these aspects in early years settings, including your own! StEPs enables a kind of 'pick-and-mix' facility for identifying provision against intentions for learning and for redressing gaps.

But, of course, this is not the full picture. Running through these issues are others associated with:

- planning;
- observation;
- effective and manageable assessment procedures;
- recording;
- progression and continuity.

All of these are covered briefly in this Pack but explored in greater depth in other related literature, including Roberts (1995), Whitebread (1996), ECEF/NCB (1998), Moriarty and Siraj-Blatchford (1998), Siraj-Blatchford (1999) and Moyles (2001). These issues we have called the 'golden threads' of early years teaching because, added to StEPs, they inform all aspects of provision intended to respect children's entitlements.

WHY THE EMPHASIS ON UNDERSTANDING CHILD DEVELOPMENT?

From birth to 7 years, children are developing as people, as learners and as citizens of our society. Education at this stage should be characterized, according to Webb (1974), by a lack of haste in a child-regarding world. Although this was written nearly three decades ago, the element of a curriculum being 'child-regarding' is still in danger of being overlooked or even forgotten in some current educational practice. The nature of children does not change between generations, although our understanding of them generally does. All aspects of child development must still be emphasized with children under 7 years (some would say throughout children's schooling; e.g. Merry 1997). Practitioners must both have and use thorough knowledge of children's growth and development if they are really to work from a basis of children's individual and collective starting points and follow this along a developmental continuum. Development, as we have conceived it in this Pack, includes:

- **social** aspects, e.g. the development of relationships with other children and adults, gaining knowledge about people in different contexts, sharing activities and experiences;
- **physical** elements, e.g. the growth in skills of movement, body awareness and control over limbs and senses; the links with psycho-motor development;
- **emotional** issues, e.g. children's feelings about themselves, about others, about the world; the growth of confidence, independence and self-esteem;
- **intellectual/cognitive** dimensions, e.g. ideas about the world and how it functions, such as number, colour, size, weight and length; the development of styles of thinking and strategies for learning; self-knowledge;
- **language and communication**, e.g. the development of spoken language and its uses; comprehension of spoken, written and body language.

This is what we have found works for us, although we recognize that there are many other ways of viewing child development and many issues such as emotional learning (see, for example, Goleman 1996) that impinge across domains. We challenged ourselves constantly with the questions, 'What does a developmental continuum look like?' and 'How can we use the idea effectively in our teaching?' We are keen to make the point, through including child development as a major focus, that the curriculum (subject-based or otherwise) must be implemented so as to *fit the developmental level of the child* rather than the current Key Stage 1 practice of shoe-horning the child into predetermined levels of subject curriculum.

There is no substitute for an in-depth knowledge of all aspects of child development, as it will inform successful teaching and learning with all children up to at least 7 years of age. As Hurst and Joseph (1998: 7) point out: 'It is the combination of this knowledge and understanding which makes it possible for the adult to help the child to move on,

so that learning and development are both enhanced'. As an example, we all know too well that the complexities involved in a 3-year-old's social development are very different from those of a normal 6-year-old and that the activities provided would equally need to be different. Three-year-olds often play *next to* other children rather than directly *with* other children. Observers will often notice from this that the play is relatively silent; in fact, children will find it difficult to talk because their brains are actively engaged in one aspect – the exploratory play – rather than in formulating language. Six-year-olds, on the other hand, often use significantly more talk in a collaborative situation where they will vie for power and control to express their own preferences.

Effective knowledge of child development, and an appreciation of the next and previous phases of education, will ensure that practitioners foster children's healthy growth and development. Without such knowledge there is a danger that practitioners will provide for 'nice' activities, rather than things that challenge young children's learning and extend their current abilities. At worst, it may lead to the provision of unsuitable paper-based activities that demand levels of concentration and physical skills that few young children possess, especially at the ages of 2, 3 and 4 years. By engaging in these developmentally inappropriate activities, children are being denied basic, underpinning experiences, concepts and skills that they will need to become competent and confident learners.

The Child Development Charts are not intended to 'type-cast' children into straight-jackets; rather, they offer practitioners a basic reminder of child development aspects so that they can estimate and work within developmental frameworks, allowing them to understand what is 'normal' progress for most children. While we know the 'average' child does not exist, all children pass through similar developmental phases and practitioners' knowledge of these enables them to be efficient and to optimize time, resources and children's life chances. Reference to these child development charts, in conjunction with StEPs, will help all practitioners to offer challenging, playful and active teaching and learning opportunities and experiences with a full knowledge of what children can achieve within each age group. Practitioner-researchers have also found these charts to be particularly helpful both in identifying children with special education needs and in setting high standards for all children.

Young children need to acquire a sense of safety and security; optimum self-esteem; a feeling that life is worth living and an ability to make sense of a range of experiences (Katz 1995: 2–3).

WHY – AND HOW – SHOULD WE PROVIDE A CURRICULUM BASED ON PLAY?

There is ample evidence from literature spanning back over 100 years that children's natural instinct to play 'feeds' their overall development, and their intellectual competence in particular (see, for example, Blakemore 2000). So we **know** that play is probably the most important activity in which young children can be engaged in these vital formative years (see Sutton-Smith 1998). We know, too, that early years practitioners have always tended to work from an intuitive belief in play as important for young children, their development and learning (Wood and Attfield 1996; Bennett et al. 1997). Observation and experience tell us we can't all be wrong, and the evidence of children's 'need' to play confronts us daily. But we have learned to live with – and to have sometimes shelved – our beliefs and are rarely required to articulate the deeper and finer points. Justifying play to others as a fundamental learning process can be difficult, particularly as there is no one clear definition of play.

The nearest we got as a group to defining play is that it is something that is fluid, flexible, ever-changing, enjoyable, serious, instinctive, active, culture-bound, a form of behaviour, a means to an end; in other words, we came to the conclusion that play and learning are rather 'messy' and non-definable. We found it impossible to categorize neatly and evaluate play as a concept or a construct and decided that 'perfect', idealized play is difficult to achieve particularly in settings associated with school, because of the accountability structures within which we all work. By 'idealized' we mean that play respects the free-choice and ownership of each child. This actually goes against the social nature and social structures of any kind of 'formalized' provision, be it a playgroup or a reception class in a school. What we were very clear about, however, was that we should strive continually to provide as near to 'perfect' play opportunities as we could.

As the following cameo shows, however, justifying play can be achieved in a variety of ways and those working through the Pack will find many examples of this type of 'good practice', helping them to justify play to others.

New parents are visiting Little Acorns Nursery. On the walls in the entrance hall are displayed labelled photographs of all those working within the setting, alongside a wide variety of information about the work and play of the nursery. Planning sheets show clearly the learning intentions behind different types of play provision. In the adjoining room, parents see captioned photographs indicating children's successful learning through play and there are a number of booklets explaining the holistic and integrated nature of learning. The children appear confident, motivated and show concentration and persistence in their activities. The parents see clear examples of how play meets children's developmental needs and the booklets enable the practitioners to answer questions explicitly and with confidence.

When explored in detail, each Statement of Entitlement to Play will support practitioners in explaining the importance of a particular kind of play associated with specific developmental needs and learning intentions. It will also help in identifying support strategies for individuals and groups of children whose development has reached certain levels or those whose progress is causing concern.

StEPs offers a range of other kinds of support to practitioners in explaining issues such as the problems with 'too much too soon' for young children. For example, particularly important within our society of late is the area of young children's social and emotional development: one of the main concerns expressed is about children's development and the links with how children learn. There is so much stress placed upon 'formalized' learning experiences and the content of the curriculum that social and other personal skills can be neglected – and positively marginalized! As one group of practitioners suggested, '*There is no time to stop and deal with behaviour issues because so much time has to be spent on content*'. Teachers and other educators bemoan the lack of any flexibility to respond to behavioural and social situations. Within StEPs, if these issues are identified either for individuals or collectively for a particular group of children, they can be explored through the model, the child development aspects and provision.

THE ESSENTIAL ROLE OF PRACTITIONERS AS CO-PLAYERS

Research over the last 30 years has shown play to be an even more powerful learning process when adults interact playfully with children (see, for example, Smilansky 1968; Smilansky and Shefatya 1990; Moyles 1994; Bruce 1998). Our experience of trying to engage in children's play, however, made us doubt whether it was possible to make inroads into children's play without changing its nature and feeling like interlopers! In early discussions, it was not unusual to hear members of the practitioner-researcher group make comments such as:

> *I found that when I tried to go into role play, that was incredibly difficult because the children almost don't accept you.*

> *I think you have to be seen as playing and I think that it's great to play, but it's a hard step for children to accept us as players.*

> *Although we set up imaginative corners, as persons in ourselves, we aren't always happy being in there and playing imaginatively. But I'm not saying that we don't provide some very nice, imaginative play.*

When we began to analyse the differences in play with and without adult engagement, however, it became very clear that **children gain significantly by engaging with respectful adults** who find sensitive ways of being part of the play. This manifested itself in many different ways, of which the following are just a few examples:

- One practitioner put out constructional toys and made her own model while playing alongside the children, at all times ensuring that she was using the language of the materials, such as colours, texture and including mathematical language, e.g. shape names, corner, edge.
- Another adult became accepted in hospital play by bringing in a bunch of silk flowers for a patient and then questioning the hospital 'staff' about the patient's condition and needs.
- A teacher observes a group of children at the water play trying to fill narrow-necked bottles from large jugs. It is evident that some children will become frustrated and the play will deteriorate. He introduces funnels and tubing and demonstrates their use.
- A group of 4-year-olds are playing in the home area and decide to make a list so as to go shopping. Hearing their intentions, the nursery nurse quickly writes some things on a list and asks the children if they can please get these items when they go shopping. This prompts the children to add their own items to the list and they identify the need to write people's names alongside items on the list.
- As part of learning about forces, a Year 1 teacher provides a number of toys. She plays with the children as they use the toys, guiding them to find out how they work.

This type of interaction increased as practitioner-researchers analysed their own and the children's reactions to different play situations and gained confidence in their ability to engage themselves at the children's level and through thinking in child-like ways. Let's be clear, however: children do not expect adults to be like large children! What they do expect is that adults will respect the play situations in which children are engaged and honour the rules that the children have inevitably evolved. The best moment of all is when the children *invite you* into the play as a character in their story – trust indeed!

Lend us your skirt!
Two children – one with a toy donkey and one with 'baby Jesus' – rush towards the nursery nurse. They ask her anxiously if they can hide the baby in her long skirt as they are escaping from King Herod. The nursery nurse sits down with the children hiding the baby in the folds of her skirt. At this point King Herod and his soldiers ride by searching unsuccessfully for the baby. The sensitivity of this intervention enabled the children to deal with their insecurities about this aspect of the story and confirmed their trust in her.

Do you have examples of when children have invited you into their play? How did you feel about being part of the play? Adults can feel uncomfortable about playing but, as these examples show, the adult role is varied, powerful and necessary in developing children holistically.

A FINAL WORD FROM THE PRACTITIONER-RESEARCHERS

Through examining play episodes like these, we increasingly recognized the processes of our own thinking and reflection on play practices and the essential nature of our playful teaching roles. One aspect of this was our desire to share with you, the readers, some of the current outcomes of our thinking. In a way, the project is on-going in that all of the practitioner-researchers continue to challenge their own – and each others' – play practices. At the last 'formal' meeting everyone was clear: *'The project has become a way of life!'*

We also know that what we have achieved is essentially dynamic. StEPs has the potential for flexible use in the hands of reflective practitioners. It will be vital that users of the Pack continually reflect and challenge themselves on their practices and provision. The key aspect for the group is the thinking process behind StEPs that enabled us to engage in reflective practices. Readers should consider how they can work collaboratively with other practitioners to cope with the inevitable challenge of evolving one's own practices to meet the needs of children and community.

It's our project and we're very much involved with it but, personally, we all probably wanted a greater understanding and awareness surrounding the issues of learning through play. I think we've all met that and more in terms of confidence in ourselves to 'deliver' and to see its purpose and identify the possibilities that are now ahead of us. We're now desperately keen and excited in what we're doing. The challenge is there and it's always [going to be] there – but it's exciting!

Share the excitement of playful teaching and learning as you make your way through the Pack and what it has to offer.

NOTE

1 The Esmée Fairbairn Charitable Trust, to whom we are indebted for their major support. The intentions and outcomes of the different phases of the research have been written up in various journals for those who would like to read a more thorough account of the underpinning research (see Adams 2000; Adams *et al.* 2000; Moyles and Adams 2000; Adams and Moyles 2000).

SECTION TWO

The practitioner-researchers: who are we and what do we do?

The group of eleven people came together under the auspices of a project initially entitled 'Too Busy to Play?' (TBtP), in which we could all explore our beliefs and values in relation to play within our roles as early years practitioners either directly in the context of settings or in providing initial and continuing professional development experiences. This section details who we all are, expressed in our own words and written in our own inimitable ways! Some of us appear on the accompanying video.

Siân Adams (Project researcher)

During my initial teacher training, I took the opportunity to pursue an additional course on child development studies. Learning more about very young children promoted an intense interest in how young children learn, especially in the school environment, and I decided to specialize in early years. This was in spite of much encouragement to move to KS2 or senior management in schools – 'You'll get into a rut in early years!'

Following a 12-year spell playing with my own children, I taught in four different schools, each post based within early years. In the later capacity of advisory teacher, I developed teaching links with two neighbouring universities. The combination of working in schools and in an academic environment helped to bridge the theory and practice gap, as well as bringing both into sharp relief.

In response to one practitioner asking, 'How can children learn through play if we are unable to teach through play?', I turned my pursuits to exploring ways in which children could, realistically, learn through play. Then I was offered the opportunity to work with the 'Too Busy to Play?' project group. One of the key aspects of working on the TBtP has been the effective, close collaborative relationship we have developed with each other. This training pack, StEPs, is the result of that work – it is written by practitioners and researchers for practitioners and researchers.

Jill Evans (Practitioner-researcher)

I am one of the two nursery nurses on the project. I am very much a nursery practitioner and respect and value children's entitlement to play. Like many of you, I know only too well the dilemmas we all face in making appropriate provision for young children and I know how useful the Pack will be in supporting people like us.

Most of the last 15 years has been spent in nurseries attached to primary schools, my current one being in an inner-city area where children come from a mix of cultural and social backgrounds. When the letter arrived from the Project Director asking me to be involved with some research into children's play, I decided that it would be interesting, as my first thought was 'No problem! I provide for children's play everyday so I must know something about it!' How 'loose' that statement feels today!

When the team of practitioner-researchers first met, it became apparent that we were united in our belief that children learn through play. However, when we came to discuss what play is, although we could agree on rather broad generalizations to do with play, we started to agonize about such issues as the difference between play and active learning. For me to try to answer the questions, I had to go back to my nursery and carry out observations. I also had to determine my role within that nursery – how much was I a player in the children's eyes or was I always the director? Without understanding these roles, I could not make my practice change. I had never been challenged before on what I believed to be 'good practice' in terms of play provision and I found it uplifting to be able to justify this.

If anything I hope you will use this Pack to help you to stand back, observe and begin to challenge your practices and, like me, begin to acquire the ability to stand up for what you know about how children learn through play. I have learned how to make others understand, for example, that an activity such as a cardboard box, glued with attachments and covered in paper, made and prepared totally by the child, entitles that child to a real holistic learning experience that no worksheet could ever do.

Helen Geisler (Practitioner-researcher)

When the StEPs project began, I was completing my MA dissertation, teaching Year 2 children full-time and was also head of KS1! I was thrilled to be invited to join the group and quickly we began to exchange ideas as to how we felt children could learn effectively and be encouraged to help generate their own learning. Over time we have evolved ways in which children can be encouraged to learn through play, exploration and shared problem-solving. I find the challenge of using the Pack to balance and broaden the Foundation Stage Guidance and the National Curriculum an evolving framework that complements and can be meshed together.

I am now in my 18th year of teaching and, as a deputy head in a new setting, find that the need to step back and evaluate my teaching remains constant. How best can I foster and develop collaborative ways in which my Year 2 children can learn? What skills do the children need? Is curriculum knowledge the main aim of teaching? How can we plan for diversity and enable children to reflect and challenge each other's ideas? I think learning through play remains *the* way forward. As practitioners our task is to identify When? How? Why? What? Where? activities take place. Being part of the group has helped me to sustain the confidence to play and learn with my children.

Liz Magraw (Practitioner-researcher)

Currently, I am the early years and art coordinator in a primary school as well as being seconded to my local Early Years Development and Childcare Partnership as a mentor teacher for the Early Years for part of the week.

After teaching the older primary range and special needs, I was requested by a previous school to transfer to Year R. I did so unconvinced and reluctant with dreams of escape, but I never looked back. I still delight in the children's enthusiasm, freshness, spontaneity and want to have a role in this crucial part of their voyage of discovery. It is THEY who keep me believing in education, education, education! They allow me to enjoy play, imagination and spontaneity myself – I can be zany, have fun, wear silly hats: I'm an early years practitioner!

That said, the seriousness of the all-encompassing responsibility that comes with the job can be overwhelming. This led me to accept the challenge of the play research project – and what a challenge it has been! It has been soul-searching, demanding, even frightening at times, but always rewarding. The special links between the individuals in this group have been forged through a very real and painful analytical process.

Originally, I had joined the group to work with like-minded people and to find a framework that would support my commitment to play as THE learning medium for children. The project has done just that, but had I known then how cathartic it was going to be, I might have hesitated: yet I have no regrets. Being part of the project has given greater depth to my conviction about the importance of an holistic approach with children. Over the years, this has been fuelled by my own daughter going through the British education system and my own very different experiences as a child going through my education in France. In 'my day', the French system was very formal but started later (and still does). But it gave me a much broader set of skills and knowledge than my British student counterparts, because specialization was not so early or so stringent. Interestingly enough, the French education system, certainly in its primary phase, is becoming less formal, less teacher-centred, adopting a more holistic and child-centred approach at a time when I perceive that English provision is becoming over-formal and inflexible!

With the knowledge I have acquired from the research project and through being part of the writing of the Pack, I and the children can confidently now play and learn.

Pat Medland (Practitioner-researcher)

I decided my career lay in working with young children when I was 17 and on holiday in Spain. On the beach each day my friends would lay, idly basting themselves in the sun, while I dug massive holes, carried water, searched out shells and hermit crabs with a small band of children seemingly accumulated from thin air. Children had this habit of attaching themselves to me and I enjoyed their company – what better way to make a living? As a result of this, I trained as an early years teacher and, during my work in nurseries, playgroups and crèches, I found out that having fun with children is quite a serious business.

At the time of joining the project, I was head of a nursery unit in an inner-city school with quite a few years of experience. However, on this project, I soon discovered that experience was not enough: I found myself struggling to articulate my principles and beliefs and questioning exactly what the children in my setting were doing. Along with all the others, I went through a time of challenge, examination and uncertainty before beginning to rebuild our thinking. For me, the six Entitlement Statements are a powerful means by which I can rationalize my principles about play.

I am at present seconded to work with private and voluntary sector providers as a Nursery Education Development Officer (and doing an MA!). Recently, while visiting a playgroup two small children climbed into my lap to talk as closely as they could to me about themselves and to touch this stranger's necklace and hair. Having established relationships, they then invited and included me in their play. This is their time, the time for fun and enjoyment in learning and playing. And it is our amazing job to take it seriously, while sharing the fun ourselves!

Janet Moyles (Project director)

My overriding passion for most of my years in teaching has been in finding out about young children and what makes them 'tick'. Part of this has been observation over many years of children's play – what they do, how they do it, what they make of it, and so on. From being a trained nursery teacher, through primary headship, a researcher role and then into higher education (initially as a lecturer and more recently as a professor), as time has gone by, my thinking (and experience) has shifted somewhat. More recently, I've become increasingly interested in the influence of adults on young children and especially on their play.

It was therefore with great joy that, in 1997, I succeeded not only in achieving funding for a project about play but that the project in itself meant that a team of high-quality practitioners would be able to engage in depth and over time in the process of exploring play, learning and adult roles. Having a full-time researcher (undertaking a PhD) attached to the project whose playful thinking has engaged and deepened my own, was yet another bonus. It has been my privilege to play and work with all the team over the period of the project and beyond. From thinking of me as 'the expert', it has been very rewarding to see and hear them engage with the issues and, in no uncertain terms, challenge some of my own assumptions and values. It has been equally satisfying to see how much reflecting on our own experiences has given all of us the confidence to articulate our views about effective play practices and the strength to express these to others.

Claire Orton (Practitioner-researcher)

I approached the writing of this autobiography by considering what I, as a reader, would want to know about someone who had contributed to a pack that set out to impact upon my own thinking and practice as a practitioner. I would be interested in knowing the reasons why any teacher would feel strongly enough about children's play and learning to work as part of a project for nearly 3 years. What had she gained and, more importantly, what could I and my colleagues expect to gain from involvement in the play research? Why should I, as a practitioner already over-burdened with the practicalities of daily working life and its accompanying paper mountain, take time to wade through yet more paper? I would also want to know that the writer was approaching both the StEPs Pack and the reader from a 'real world' context.

The school I currently work in as a nursery teacher serves a large council estate in the City of Leicester and was subject to 'special measures' following an OfSTED inspection in November 1997. Four inspections later, it finally came out of special measures in May 1999. The school has had a turbulent history in many ways – and is definitely part of the real world!

When I joined the play research group in October 1997, all I knew was that I was interested in play and its links with children's learning, but I certainly did not know what to expect of the project. At the time, as a busy teacher with a management role in the school and with the first inspection looming, my time was spent in attending meetings, filling in paperwork and organizing children, adults and resources. It was NOT spent in reflection on my own practice or my level of knowledge or, more challenging still, having other early years practitioners reflecting on my practice and level of knowledge!

Only a few weeks into the project, myself and several other members of the group entered what we call our 'black hole'. Just exactly what WERE we doing with the children everyday? Were they playing, learning actively or working? Was I intervening too much or too little? Was my planning too rigid or too open-ended? Surely I was a successful and experienced practitioner, so why couldn't I articulate exactly what I was doing and why? I instinctively 'knew' how young children learn and how to move their learning forward – didn't I?

As the play project progressed, I was reassured about my practice but challenged by gaps in my own knowledge. It was inspiring that there was a group of people with a voice, willing to stand up for what children are entitled to in terms of play and learning. I was strengthened by the depth of thinking behind what became StEPs and this gave me the power to justify why children must and will learn in playful ways with playful adults.

Debbie Pentecost (Practitioner-researcher)

I work as a nursery nurse in a large county primary school as a member of the nursery team. We work very much on a 'learning through play' basis throughout the whole early years department and all operate in the fundamental belief that children are entitled to learn through play experiences. Being part of the play project has enabled me to reflect upon my own and others' practice, and to take time to observe, share and assess children's play and learning with colleagues in order to inform future planning.

Being part of the TBtP Project has given me the confidence and conviction to stand on my 'soap box' and not only to justify playing but to explain to other adults – whether they are parents, colleagues who teach older children or visiting 'others' – how and why we play, its importance, structure and spontaneity. However busy other adults are, I believe that they should never be 'too busy to play', for there is no better means for enabling a child to learn, enjoy learning and want to keep on learning than through the medium of play.

Sue Gray (Practitioner-researcher)

Three years ago when I was asked to take part in the TBtP Project, I was both delighted and enthusiastic to contribute, but never really imagined how much work the project would be, how much it would influence my work or how satisfying it would become.

I attended the first few meetings thinking I had a secure knowledge of children's play, having taught in early years since 1983 and in a nursery for the last 12 years. How wrong I was! The analysis of our practice made me question what the children were really learning. Despite the constant demands and changes placed on education and the ever-increasing paperwork, I can never escape the reason I decided to teach – the children! I still enjoy their spontaneity and the pleasure they experience in so much of what they do. They never cease to have an appetite for new things and the opportunities given to them. Most of all, I love their ability to 'sum up' in their own language the obvious, and their thoughts about the world and the people in it.

Vivien Robins (Practitioner-researcher)

When the TBtP Project began, I was working as the lead teacher in an 80-place 4+ unit of a Leicestershire primary school. What particularly interested me was the opportunity to deepen my knowledge of child development and explore in detail how the play of 4- and 5-year-old children may or should differ from that of younger or older children.

Having already completed a masters degree, at the start of the play research project I was studying part-time for a doctorate in education. Two years into the project, I became senior lecturer in Early Years Education at De Montfort University with the new role of teacher trainer at its Bedford campus.

The play research informed my (now completed) doctoral research and school practice significantly as well as giving me good 'ammunition' to make responses to government early years consultations. It has also led to my involving all my family, for example my husband has listened, shopped, cooked and almost turned into a 4+ practitioner himself as he has become involved in my continual anecdotes about 'my 4-year-olds' and my colleagues on the play project. When he unpacked some new computer equipment, he even showed me, rather excitedly, the convoluted polystyrene packing and said 'You could use this really well in sand play!' So the messages about play and good early years practice touch a wide variety of people, as I feel it should.

Gillian Simpson (Practitioner-researcher)

Three years ago when the project began, I was working part-time as a nursery teacher in a 60-place inner-city nursery in a Leicester primary school. What particularly interested me was the opportunity to share successes and failures in relation to play-based teaching and learning practices, which I feared was becoming overlooked and pushed out of existence by an ever-demanding conformity to National Curriculum expectations.

I qualified as a 3–8 specialist teacher in 1982 and initially elected to be a reception class teacher. It was with a certain degree of trepidation that I eventually assumed the 'mantle' of nursery teacher, I have to say that a few parents thought this was a backward step! How could I develop and personalize the nursery without seeming to devalue or denigrate the domain of my predecessor?

When I joined the play research group, I had also become a parent. Having a child with a Statement of Special Educational Needs has focused my attention on differentiation. How can we provide a play and learning curriculum in a safe and secure environment that can be accessed by all children at different levels of development? The first few meetings allowed us the opportunity to compare and contrast our embedded beliefs. We were constantly asked to challenge assumptions and surmount intuition and 'gut' feelings. I personally struggled with questioning everything that I had held so highly.

As the project developed into StEPs, we all became reassured and committed to this way forward. We had found a vehicle for playing and learning – our Entitlements. StEPs encompasses all that is good in creating a mutually beneficial curriculum for adult and child which celebrates the right to play and learn and the empowerment that brings.

SECTION THREE

Using the materials within the Pack: let the children – and practitioners – play!

The aims of this section are to:
- Explore the rationale behind the Pack in terms of its use.
- Explain different ways in which the Pack materials might be used to promote practitioner reflection on play practices.

It may be self-evident to many of you who read this Pack that we hold clearly to the view that young children must be respected and valued for who they are and what they represent; in other words, they are vital young PEOPLE with views, ideas and feelings just like the rest of us, who impact in a variety of ways upon the world. For children to gain a self-concept that involves self-esteem, self-confidence and self-knowledge, adults must show children – through, for example, playing with them, spending time with them and responding to them as worthy partners – that they understand and relate to children learning not only the content and context of lifelong education, but independence and opportunities for responsible choice.

In the Introduction to *All Our Futures* (DfEE 1999: 9), Ken Robinson asserts:

> Policy makers everywhere emphasize the urgent need to develop human resources and, in particular, to promote creativity, adaptability and better powers of communication. We argue that this means reviewing some of the basic assumptions of our education system.

Within this Pack, we argue that creativity, flexibility and the ability to make connections are implicit within high-quality play, learning and curriculum experiences for children (see also Early Years Curriculum Group 1998). The role of respectful educators is to provide, model, encourage, interact, inform and nurture such characteristics in children (Nutbrown 1996). Without this combination, young children's current and future learning experiences and understanding will not grow and develop in the way that societies need and demand. Given the strictures and some erroneous expectations that are implicit within part of the National Literacy and Numeracy Strategies, it is beholden on all early childhood educators – practitioners, parents and carers – to engage with young children's needs and interests.

It is well known that young children learn most effectively from those experiences and activities that interest them and to which they can readily relate from aspects of their everyday lives (ECEF/NCB 1998). It is easy to see how difficult – even impossible – this is likely to be in a class of 4- to 5-year-olds. For example, in physical development, these children may span a range from the 'average' 2- to 3-year-old to a child with motor skills equivalent to an 'average' 9- to 10-year-old (dependent on development and maturation). In cognitive development terms, an able 4- to 5-year-old could be undertaking scientific experiments well into KS2 content. A linguistically capable child of a similar age may have a reading age 5 years in advance of chronological age! This does not mean, of course, that the child should be treated as a 10-year-old! Socially, the same child may only communicate at an average level and may be emotionally insecure.

The message is 'All children are different' and if, as practitioners, we are showing respect for them as individuals, our practices must reflect such differentiation. The child development charts in Section 8 offer a guide to considering the differential needs of children from around 3 years of age upwards. Age-defined statements need to be handled with caution but do offer some guidance as to what might be expected generally of children within a specific year group.

This is the strength and joy of the Pack. It is possible to begin in different places for different purposes either considering children's learning and developmental needs or practitioners' knowledge and teaching. It is even possible to start with resources or a curriculum subject.

Essentially, we intend that the Pack should be used for continuing professional development activities. The Statements of Entitlement are the cornerstones with the video, curriculum links and cameo-based explanations providing exemplification through highlighting the meaning behind the StEPs. The Pack can be used in conjunction with any other curriculum guidance materials and, indeed, links particularly well with the Foundation Stage Guidance.

HOW MIGHT THE PACK BE APPROACHED?

Apart from straightforwardly reading it like a book and watching the video for the joy of seeing children and adults playing, you might also:

1 Read the Introduction in conjunction with the Statements of Entitlement before viewing the video to discuss aspects of children's play and the practitioners' roles.
2 View the video first and decide on the answers to the questions posed, then work through the Entitlements and, perhaps, child development charts to identify what has been characterized

USING THE MATERIALS WITHIN THE PACK

within the video and the relationship with practice.

3. Read through some of the cameo stories relating to the entitlements in Sections 6 and 7 and then refer back to the entitlement and child development charts to establish your understanding of how the various elements link together and might inform your own planning and provision.

4. Look through some of the planning sheets provided (or through your own planning sheets) and relate these to the entitlement charts.

5. Each setting will identify a variety of needs each time new children arrive or as the existing group develops through the academic year. The overall entitlement charts can provide general guidance through, for example, giving an overview of physical development through meaningful activities.

6. Watch the video and respond to the questions raised. Link your responses back to StEPs.

7. Take one of the Entitlements that interests you most and think of all the ways in which you might implement this with the children through one or more aspects of development. Add to your own lists aspects from that entitlement's chart and plan for some teaching and learning.

8. Reflect on your own practice as you explore others' practice, in the cameos and video. Use this to identify your own learning requirements, changes you might plan to make or aspects of your practice you wish to retain or develop.

9. Identify just one area of your classroom, e.g. the home corner or construction area. Use StEPs to help you evaluate this one area in terms of provision and the ways in which children's learning might be enriched.

10. Identify one area of child development. StEPs will refresh and update your knowledge and understanding of how children develop and learn. The detailed information in the StEPs columns will suggest ways in which you can apply that knowledge and understanding to your practice and use it to inform planning, observations and assessment.

Further ways of using the video and linking across elements of the Pack are explained and explored in Section 4.

Another way of using the Pack is through considering your own or the children's needs. For example, to help you identify what you need and when, you might pose yourself a series of questions and find responses in the Pack, such as:

- What do I like doing best with these children? Look at columns E and F across the six Entitlements to extend your thinking and decision-making. This may well lead to the following questions: What should we provide more of for this particular intake of children? Do some of the children require more opportunities for trial-and-error learning (Entitlement 2) to promote collaboration and recognition of their own and others' ideas?

- How useful is our Baseline and other methods of assessment? Explore the contents of column A across the six Entitlements. From this you can establish some aspects of children's likely prior knowledge that might warrant assessment and check these against what your Baseline scheme requires.

- How often, and in what form, should feedback to parents or carers be? Discuss the contents of column C as a likely source of providing relevant information.

- Look at your medium-term planning sheet and examine these against the six Entitlements. Do you need to make more provision for a specific Entitlement? Do you need to widen the materials you offer in a variety of contexts?

- Think about how often parents, carers and other adults help in your setting. In what ways do they work with children? Do they contribute to all aspects of children's development (column B), thus valuing the child's holistic development rather than just cognitive development? Under column F, what might they offer within any areas in which their contribution is not made?

- Have we thought enough about personal and social development? Look through all six charts across 'Social' in column B and decide whether there are any other activities that could be promoted. Alternatively, as Entitlement 1 is all about social development, read through the whole of that chart and see what types of play and learning might be provided.

As can be seen, these different activities using the Pack will take anything from 10 minutes to an hour or more. Those who have piloted the Pack have found that users get 'hooked' into different aspects and whatever time-scale we offer will be overridden in use!

The next section explores further the use of the video.

SECTION FOUR

Using the video: what we can learn by observing children and practitioners playing

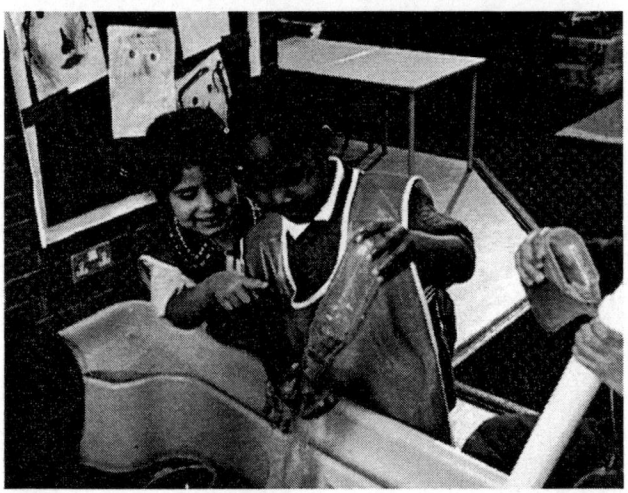

The aims of this section are to:
- Explain the contents and background of the video accompanying the Pack.
- Describe the various elements of the video and how it links to the StEPs.
- Outline what the video clips are intended to show by way of meeting children's needs and the role of playful practitioners.
- Delight and challenge you through scenes from everyday settings.

Video duration: Approximately 35 minutes
Background: Six practitioner-researchers within the group planned an activity in which children are learning through play (see Table 4.1)
Content: Six short play scenes or cameos based on one area of children's development, refined to one aspect of the classroom
Curriculum: One specified area of learning often informing many

Through the video, we invite you into our classrooms to show you StEPs in action. There is always a delight in seeing other people's settings and ways of working and this video is no exception. In most cases, you will see the classrooms just as they are. In a few cases, it was necessary to 'set up' the filming, for example, there was no room in the smaller settings for practitioners, all the children, visitors, the camera, microphones and Jon and Carl (the video operators and producers) without making the children feel overwhelmed, inhibited or self-conscious.

Once the activities had been planned and set up, it was important that the children responded as spontaneously as is usual for young children. Mainly, we wanted to capture the warmth, the humour and seriousness, the naturalness of children, the spontaneity of play, the reality of daily practice and, in particular, evidence of teaching and learning through play.

It is hoped that the final film is a fair and true representation of what occurs daily in classrooms. Some of the play activities continued for up to one hour, but for the purposes of this training pack they have been reduced to less than 5 minutes each. We considered it would be more useful to see a few minutes of video that captured specific aspects of teaching and learning rather than hours of detail that might detract from the main purpose of each clip – to show you each of the Entitlements in practice. The text is also dotted with a few questions for you to consider about the practitioner's role and professional knowledge.

For example, Cameo 1, 'Debbie and the Aliens!', focuses on:

- Entitlement 1
- in the area of children's social and linguistic development
- at the writing table
- during a Literacy lesson.

However, within Cameo 1 you will also see examples of Maths, Knowledge and Understanding of the World, Science, and so on. In reality, children do not learn in neat, tidy, predictable chunks, so frequently many of the Entitlements are represented in several cameos. Equally children do not necessarily develop in single, easily identifiable domains. For example, although Debbie has planned to promote children's linguistic development, you will also see evidence of their social development in the chatter and laughter of their work. However, for the purposes of the video, we have focused on one area of development. For similar reasons, we will focus on just one area of the curriculum. You have the chance to identify other 'incidental' areas of learning and development according to your own knowledge and understanding and this will be useful in getting to know what the video has to

Table 4.1 Plan for video

	Entitlement	Development	Curriculum	Activity
Cameo 1: Debbie and the Aliens!	1	Social and Linguistic	Language and Literacy Knowledge and Understanding Numeracy	Writing area
Cameo 2: Eid Party	2	Emotional	Language/Literacy	Role play
Cameo 3: Kieran Dieran	3	Linguistic	Linguistic: Speaking and Listening	Creative area
Cameo 4: Incy Wincy	4	Intellectual	Science	Water area
Cameo 5: Building Houses	5	Intellectual	Numeracy	Construction: Lego
Cameo 6: (a) The Hedgehog (b) Blast Off	6	Intellectual and Physical	Technology	Construction: (a) Creative area (b) Outside area

offer you and other practitioners within your setting. The more you watch it, the more you will 'see'!

There are a number of ways in which you can use the video. In this section, each one of the cameos is approached differently to demonstrate the versatility of using the video to support training, reflective practice or evaluation of existing practice. There is no best way to work with this. We suggest you:

- read through this section,
- view the video, and then
- decide which approach will best suit your needs or preferences.

You may well invent other ways of using it!

We also suggest that first you just watch the video to get an overall feel for its messages and the links with other aspects of StEPs. Some aspects are amusing, some very serious. Each cameo contains snippets of activities, although there is also a 'story' to hold it together. Within that story there are several threads of other activities and aspects of learning. These only become visible after you have seen the video at least once. The various levels of activity are pointed out in the text that follows, describing each cameo, and each one concludes with information on the planning undertaken by the practitioner, including an evaluation of the activity. Of necessity, these plans are all different – you can choose whether this particular type of planning would be helpful for you. We have not tried to 'sanitize' the plans: they are as produced by practitioners for their everyday way of dealing with this crucial issue. You are free to challenge them and learn from their idiosyncrasies!

But first, view the video. Enjoy the children, then return for more serious, professional study.

VIDEO – ENTITLEMENT 1

Debbie and the Aliens!

Young children are entitled to play experiences that engage them affectively and socially in their own and others' learning

Literacy lesson, promoting children's linguistic development

This Entitlement begins with column A: ***Children's development and prior learning***.

Social development

These children are very interested in space and aliens. Space themes often appear in their play, with their use of construction materials, a favourite space story from the book corner or just chatting with friends in a quiet corner of the classroom or playground. Debbie has capitalized on this interest by using 'space adventure' (Binns-McDonald 1999) as a stimulus for further discussion and activities throughout the day. This story can also be a starting point for other aspects of the curriculum as well as building on their current interest in literacy. This introductory lesson is interactive, rooted in children's related interests, which the children have brought into the situation. Debbie encourages the children to contribute their own ideas to the story, especially as the concept of aliens is probably outside any concrete, familiar experiences they have had outside school! Talking about their own interests and experiences of space stories, and relating this to other stories they have enjoyed, helps them to visualize the setting for today's 'space adventure'. Debbie needs to be sure that all the children are engaged in this theme and not just the children who are more articulate or assertive. The children have been at school for two terms, during which time they have learned to contribute to and listen to small group discussions. They are able to work on their own and in a group setting – look at the earnest, concentrated expressions on their faces; each one tells a story!

Prior learning: language and literacy

Within the domain of linguistic development they have learned to express their own thoughts and ideas; some have learned to listen, to talk about their experiences and to engage in discussion. Debbie's professional understanding and knowledge about these children enables her to ask differentiated questions to ensure interest is sustained and the children are challenged.

> TO THINK ABOUT...
> Can you identify the specific knowledge the practitioner needs to identify and interpret children's existing skills?

Following the story, the children are invited to work in smaller groups, which provides additional focused opportunity for the children to listen to each other and to engage in imaginative discussion about the space world they are creating. The group setting, the resources and an interested adult provide a structure for their developing ideas and feelings. Having one large piece of paper to draw on encourages a large collaborative piece of work – look how the space ships travel across each other's territory! They use the resources to take their aliens on a journey, plan the route, encounter a range of galactic adventures, and even count the aliens' fingers.

Debbie provides opportunities for them to use imaginative and 'extraterrestrial' language from the text, within different contexts:

- in a large group while they are listening to and discussing the story;
- in a smaller focused group activity where they use the information they have gleaned from the story;
- in a large group discussion when the children talk about what they have been doing, taking the opportunity to apply and communicate their knowledge in yet another context.

She also refers to the story she has just read and encourages them to recollect the events; she later makes links with other stories. Having an appreciative audience serves to develop their confidence as they learn to respect each other. They listen to each other chat playfully about the ideas they have generated during their work together, sharing ideas about 22-fingered aliens bouncing around on their bottoms!

Moving across the columns of StEPs guides the adult's further planning for teaching. Use StEPs to help determine other ways in which you might develop the children's literacy skills.

> TO THINK ABOUT...
> 1 How do you feel this also supported children's social and emotional development, for example the ways in which they might be sensitive to the needs of others?
> 2 There are opportunities within this cameo to make links with other areas of learning: Knowledge and Understanding of the World, and Numeracy. Why might this be desirable?

VIDEO – ENTITLEMENT 2

Eid Party

Young children are entitled to play experiences that are set in meaningful and relevant activities and contexts for learning

Role play, with opportunities for emotional development and developmental writing

This Entitlement begins with column E: *Practitioners will make provision...*

Pat has made provision for a child-sensitive classroom through using evidence about children's cultural, social, religious and ethnic background. Her knowledge of the community, the families, the children and their diverse cultures has provided her with sufficient information to ensure the children's home backgrounds, cultures and customs are reflected in the provision for role-play. The children have a strong sense of self. They know about the various customs and are familiar with the significance and purpose of the wide range of resources in their home corner. They explore frequently the range of resources throughout the classroom, make choices and use them to develop their own play.

The writing area is equipped with appropriate resources to design and write party invitations. The children know they are free to find their friends and deliver the invitations.

> TO THINK ABOUT...
> How might Pat have acquired this information about the children's cultural and ethnic background?

The children spend very little time engaged in exploratory play. They know how to access the materials, understand their purposes, how to care for them and how to put them away when they have finished their task or when their play moves on to another area in the classroom.

Emotional development

Pat has provided activities and situations that allow the children to demonstrate and build on what they

Debbie's short-term activity plan

Prior learning
To promote further development, children need opportunities to engage in discussion in different social contexts, which will enable them to use their listening skills, questioning skills, and how to operate within a group to build their own confidence and respect the views of others.

Plan
Aim: To develop children's linguistic skills when operating as part of a small group using discussion and communicating ideas verbally and on paper.

Previous learning
Each week the children have used a story or poem as a stimulus for the week's focus, e.g. 'Whatever Next' by Jill Murphy. They have also used a role play area, a space rocket and mission control centre, thus creating a variety of contexts for language and communication skills to develop.

Learning objectives
How to interact and cooperate with one another
To listen to the ideas of others
To use imaginative and creative ideas and skills
Make own choices and decision
To use new vocabulary

Resources
Story: 'Space adventure'
Black sugar paper
Crayons and chalks
Clip art prints
Blu-Tack

Evaluation
The children found the space topic fascinating. This was the final week and the 'space adventure' story had been chosen as the stimulus for the activity. The children immediately engaged in conversation with each other, sharing ideas and listening to each other. The practitioner supported the children's learning by taking part as a 'map-maker', questioning and challenging the children, offering new vocabulary and valuing the children's ideas and drawings. The children that chose to come to this activity (with one exception) are quite articulate and all enjoy drawing and writing and are extremely creative as story-tellers, which is probably why the lesson went well and the children remained focused and enthusiastic for some considerable time.

already know about their own and others' cultures and religions. They are very confident in their play. Mohammed confidently walks to the sink to do *wazu* (Muslim ritual of washing and cleansing) before joining the party. The children nearby accept and respect his play. Nobody was challenged: the differences are respected and understood. This, in turn, encourages the children to take ownership of their play, leading to highly motivated learning. Within the theme of the 'Eid Party', the children were given the choice of what preparations to make, again encouraging ownership and independence of thought. The children's enthusiasm and motivation were used to develop their concentration and perseverance. The party food made by the children includes biriani and sweets such as burfi and dhadu, accompanied on this occasion by crisps, cheese and potatoes, representing all the children's favourite fare!

> TO THINK ABOUT...
> 1 In what ways do the resources support the learning intention, which is to ensure that children problem solve and carry out the planning of the Eid Party?
> 2 What else might the practitioner do to encourage the children to value and respect those who are different from them?

Language and literacy

The purpose of the activity is clearly stated at the beginning: 'Today we're going to have an Eid Party'. This provides a meaningful context for the children to write their own party invitations. We see evidence of children's writing, reading and communicating with each other. Pat has planned time to intervene in this play so she can support

Pat's playful short-term learning plan

Date: 30.11.99   **Name**: Pat Medland

Children are entitled to:
1 play experiences that engage them affectively and socially in their own and others' learning
2 play experiences that are set in meaningful and relevant activities and contexts for learning ✓
3 play experiences that promote curiosity and the use of imagination and creativity in learning
4 engage in play experiences that are open-ended and offer trial-and-error learning without fear of failure
5 playful, exploratory and experiential activities with a variety of materials and resources and within a variety of contexts
6 engage in individual and dynamic play and learning experiences relevant to their age group and stage of development

P&S ✓   L&L ✓   Ma   K&U   Cr ✓   Ph ✓

Aims:
To build children's self-awareness, identity and self-esteem
To learn about ways of celebrating Eid
To participate by individual contributions to a group activity
To have fun as a group!

Activity:
Discussion of religions and ways of celebrating – Muslim, Hindu and Christian. Eid Party – what do we need to do?
Choice of activity – making food (in way children choose)
   – making invitations
   – dressing up
   – preparing in home corner
     ritual washing/prayers

Children: Ind.   Group ✓   Free Choice
                              all of group 1

Adult role:
Instigate activity
Support self-initiated activities
Reinforce main points of activity

Evaluation:
Children have a good awareness of what religion they belong to and that others may belong to a different religion
N – very interested in making invitations – emergent writing, mostly letters
M – Expressed his understanding of his faith clearly by his absorbed washing and prayers
All children loved dressing up to take part, not just the girls. The activities were the main focus – the actual party lasted only a short while, activities lasted up to 15–20 mins
Follow-up – Other types of parties and celebrations. Do parents have any home videos?

and guide their writing. Other adults also support the children's speaking and listening, a vital strategy used in the setting to support the children, most of whom are using English as an additional language. The children's preparation for their party is truly valued: at the end of the lesson they meet together for their celebrations. The children accept the seriousness of this. Hajim brings his mobile 'phone with him 'just in case' and the adult reminds them all of the accompanying responsibilities: 'And someone's got to do the washing up!' Consequently, opportunities for learning are highly meaningful and relevant.

VIDEO – ENTITLEMENT 3

Kieran Dieran

Young children are entitled to play experiences that promote curiosity and the use of imagination and creativity in learning

Creative activity, with opportunities for linguistic and social development (turn-taking)

This Entitlement begins with column C: ***Children need to learn...***

Linguistic development

Very young children need authentic, meaningful and relevant experiences to promote language development. Following their interest in living things, Sue has planned to support the children through observing and encouraging them to talk about the tropical fish in their classroom. Recent observations have provided evidence of children beginning to talk about interesting experiences within the classroom and the children clearly benefit from focused, sustained opportunities for conversation. Sue promotes further curiosity through providing opportunities for children to take responsibility for the fish, extending that interest with related picture books – fiction and non-fiction – and computer software.

Speaking and listening

Sue intends to provide opportunities for them to listen to each other in a context where talk is valued and respected and children can share ideas and new experiences playfully. Working in circles helps to enhance self-esteem through offering equal status and equal value to all children. They are encouraged to think, listen, talk and generally communicate. Having an adult to listen and respond to their chatter increased their sense of self-worth and motivation to contribute to the discussion. Kieran listens to Sue explaining that the fish without eyes would bump into the sides of the fish tank. He notes a gentle humour in this, repeats Sue's phrases and makes them his own. The round table, the nearby fish tanks and other related activities support the children's concentration, learning and development in this area.

Having an adult to listen to, and support, their discussion encourages the children to play and have fun with words. The sounds of 'Kieran Dieran' both amuse and delight as they begin to experiment with sounds and familiar words. They get pleasure from playing with language, through varying their voice and knowing that language may be spoken in different ways, sometimes reflecting current television favourites: '*Oh man, I've got to wipe that...*'

They play with new ideas: '*I've got 20 of those... I've got sharks... and it's called Yarky Barky... and one is R2D2*'. A supportive audience encourages them to play with words and talk imaginatively as they visualize the fish swimming: '*Bump, bump, bang on the fish tank*'.

> TO THINK ABOUT...
> - How might Sue extend the children's vocabulary and develop phonic awareness?
> - Study the lesson plan for this activity. How might you evaluate this activity?

Sue's daily learning plan

Nursery daily planning sheet	**Date:** 23 February

Area of learning: (highlight as appropriate)
Creative
Mathematics
Literacy: provide opportunities for children to talk, to express their feelings and interest in the new fish tank
Physical
Knowledge and Understanding
Personal and Social

Supported by
Teacher – encourage expressive language, promote positive self-image. Sustain, listen to and encourage children's talk
Nursery nurse
Classroom assistant
Student
Parent

Grouping by: ability, mixed ability, whole class, individual, self-selected
Small Group – work with small group – focus on promoting positive self-image, sit around table, near fish tank. Spend first part of lesson with the children around the fish tank, encouraging them to observe and talk with each other, and then move to small tables for choice of creative resources.

Aims and objectives
To build on previous experience and interests. Promote confidence in expressing opinions.
Adult to listen and encourage children's expressive language. Ask open-ended questions if appropriate to stimulate further discussion.

Evaluation
Children showing signs of being able to cope with increasing group size with adult support, and beginning to relate activities to their own experiences. They are showing respect for the feelings and thoughts of others.

VIDEO – ENTITLEMENT 4

Incy Wincy

Young children are entitled to engage in play experiences that are open-ended and offer trial-and-error learning without fear of failure

Imaginative activity with singing, storying, language and social development

This Entitlement begins with columns D and F: *Practitioners need to understand* ... and *Practitioners should teach* ...

Intellectual development

A sound understanding of how children learn underpins this play activity. Gillian has used the children's interest in music to introduce and extend a meaningful context for investigative play. Her learning objectives are embedded in a purposeful activity that makes sense to the children. She has planned to provide opportunities for children to play and to recognize and solve problems. They play together, not only solving the immediate problems that are presented to them but also creating their own problems, engaging in the fun and excitement of discovery: *'Oh look, I make water bigger!'*

This video starts with Gillian providing a meaningful context for children's water play. Singing one of their favourite songs creates a culture of confidence and fun. The children are familiar with the routines for water play and know they are expected to select their own resources. Today these are from a nearby selection of pipes, tubes and U-bends. In spite of all Gillian's planning, the children still have opportunities to be spontaneous and to take the play and learning down unexpected channels.

It is important that the adult observes and encourages but she also needs to teach! Gillian's lesson plan identifies the ideas, concepts and knowledge to be taught. When the learning outcomes are clear and focused, the teaching is more likely to be focused.

Observe how the children are finding out for themselves, making sense of their discoveries through their own thinking, hypothesizing and predicting. The excitement, motivation, stimulation and their joy of learning is very evident and we can see how their delight helps to sustain concentration and engagement with this activity: *'Now my spider's going backwards!'*

Gillian sometimes reminds the children to recall their past experience with water play. Praise and reassurance encourages them to progress with their own ideas. She continues to support their learning through scaffolding and offering guided participation. Presenting the task, one stage at a time, ensures the children are not overloaded with too much information or too many instructions: *'See if you can lift it up without the water coming out'*.

Gillian offers help when they appear to struggle, then steps back to allow the child to complete the task independently, transferring responsibility from the teacher to the child, while reminding them of the learning goal: *'Where would you like to put the spider?'* They are challenged through experimenting with new materials. Gillian responds to their requests to participate and articulates their observations: *'The spider is stuck'*. The children are learning to learn, developing metacognition and exploring their own affective responses: *'That one's scaring me!'*.

> **TO THINK ABOUT...**
> Discuss the ways in which the children's learning was influenced by Gillian's intervention. In particular, what are the benefits to children's learning when they play in small groups?

Gillian's Medium-Term Plan is rather different from the others: as well as an overall learning plan, Gillian has chosen to show how this one small-group time activity links in with the many other activities planned around the theme of nursery and finger rhymes.

Gillian's short-term learning plan

Activity	Incy wincy spider
Curriculum area	Science
Organization	Small group of children, range of materials to support investigative play in water. Place table nearby so children can make informed choice from appropriate materials: pipes, tubes and U-bends
Development	INTELLECTUAL DEVELOPMENT
Learning goals	Through play, learn to recognize and resolve problems. No outcomes expected – provide trial and error – children discover their own problems to resolve
Principle	Young children are entitled to engage in play experiences that are open-ended and offer trial-and-error learning without fear of failure
Resources	Water tray, spiders, pipes, jugs, containers
Activity	Set context following their musical interests (keen musicians in this group) singing a favourite Incy Wincy. Play with Incy and the water pipes
Evaluation	Children made their own discoveries, shared their excitement in the changing properties of water and its effect on Incy Wincy. They were able to predict how the water would flow. Evidence of peer support in problem-solving
Adult role	Use children's ideas to guide independent problem-solving

Gillian's nursery small-group medium-term plan

10.45–11.15	Language and Literacy	Mathematics	Music/Dance/Drama	Creative Development	Physical/K&U
28 Feb I'm a little teapot	S&L tea, teapot, safety, write if like or dislike tea	S&L pairs and things that go together, e.g. knife and fork. Play pairs game	Tea party game	Observational drawing of teapot. Make cups in dough. How many cups to fill a bottle of water	Make and taste different teas
6 March Mix a pancake Incy Wincy Hickory Dickory Little Miss Muffet	S&L up, down and fears, why did mouse run down clock? Draw/write something up and down	How many legs do spiders have? Discuss, look at pictures and plastic ones. Make model spiders from bricks	Personalized nursery rhymes. NP5 mouse ran up the clock	Make spider and web collage. Make spiders in dough	S&L where water goes, look for 'water spouts' and drains. Where do puddles go?
13 March Row, row, row the boat 5 Currant buns Baker's shop	Practise writing own name, correct formation Look for magnetic letters from name	Add and subtract buns NP6	Drama – boat trip. Sing 5 currant buns with props	What would you like in your sandwich and Sam's sandwich. Children make and eat sandwiches	Make boat using outdoor equipment. S&L different boats and how powered
20 March Humpty Dumpty	S&L Humpty Dumpty rhyme, who makes us better? Make get well card	Work together to build a striped wall for Humpty, high, low, long, short	Mime Humpty Dumpty. Name that nursery rhyme	Print and paint Humpty Dumpty on wall. Make Humpty from dough	Compare raw and fried eggs. List similarities and differences. Whisk white, discuss changes
27 March Counting rhymes	S&L Mother's Day. Make and write in Mother's Day card	Recongize order and write numbers 0–10. Number rhymes, 5 eggs and 5 eggs	NP12 Use percussion instruments, copy a simple rhythm	Cutting and sticking 5 currant buns on a plate	Throwing into the Easter Bunny's mouth. Throwing and catching
3 April	Read and discuss Goldilocks, what have children done that was naughty? Why? What happened? Write and draw	Make and taste porridge. Discuss like/dislike. Set table for bears' breakfast	Read Goldilocks, drama of story all children taking part	Paint picture of 3 bears, focus on size	Hand washing/smell of soaps, relate to story
10 April Easter	No small group time. A full week of Easter activities including Easter nests, cards, nests and eggs from dough, writing patterns on egg-shaped paper, cutting egg shapes, egg hunt, throwing bean bags in Easter bunny's mouth, painting with pastel colours, Easter bonnets and hot cross buns				

VIDEO – ENTITLEMENT 5

Building Houses

Young children are entitled to playful, exploratory and experiential activities with a variety of materials and resources and within a variety of contexts

Mathematics session using constructional materials

This Entitlement begins with column D: *From their professional knowledge and understanding practitioners will know...*

Mathematical development

Jill has been teaching the concept of size and developing children's spatial awareness. She is now linking this lesson to the children's recent interest in each other's homes and houses. She knows that, in the context of meaningful playful activities, children will explore the mathematical concepts contained in them, particularly so in construction play.

She gives clear instructions: *'We are going to build some houses'*. The resources are prepared at developmentally appropriate levels. The bricks and the 'building homes' theme provides a context for their play, especially important for children within the group who have special educational needs. Jill reminds the children of the range of construction materials available to them and encourages them to make choices. Mathematical language is modelled in this introduction: *'Big wooden bricks'*.

Jill spends a few moments providing suggestions, listening to the children's ideas, and building on them until she is sure the children understand the purpose of the activity and are confident and ready to play. The resources have been organized to optimize the carpet area so that children can sit in groups or lie across their buildings, to discuss their constructions with each other, play independently or collaboratively. During their play, Jill encourages the children to talk about their ideas, restating some of the phrases, providing verbal accompaniment to their actions and answering their questions: *'Is this a long one?'* – *'Yes, it is'*. This leads to Kerry's obvious delight when she similarly discovers: *'There's a big one!'*

Jill moves among the groups of children, questioning, encouraging, stepping back, observing, suggesting and challenging as the children estimate, measure, construct, take risks, solve problems. Her role is critical in ensuring the children use and apply mathematical concepts. This play activity gives purpose, meaning and relevance to her teaching.

The plenary discussion reveals children drawing on their own understanding to make sense of the world: *'Only the wind could blow down a house!'*

The second half of this cameo shows Jill with an older group of children exhibiting a broad range of developmental aspects of block play – vertical and horizontal linear, vertical and horizontal aerial, enclosure, volumetric and three-dimensional enclosure (Athey 1994).

> **TO THINK ABOUT...**
> Can you identify the ways in which the children's play in these two cameos has developed?

Look at Carl's preference for angled bricks. He has built a table in the centre of this large house and firmly rejects any rounded objects, even trying to square the cross block! The division of labour is seamless as in unspoken negotiation the children build a house, then furnish it with a rectangular table.

> **TO THINK ABOUT...**
> - How might our understanding of children's schema development inform our understanding and planning for children's learning, in particular teaching Numeracy?
> - Examine the video and discuss the ways in which the resources, in particular the types of construction materials, influence the way in which children play together.

Jill's lesson plan

Activity Title: Building Houses **Where:** in classroom, clear large space to enable children to work and discuss their projects		**Learning goals:** Maths: size, spatial awareness			
Affective and social Meaningful and relevant Imagination and creativity Trial and error Exploratory and experiential Individual and dynamic	Activity (Please note differentiated activities/assessment opportunities/ deployment of staff) Following a walk to see some of our houses, discuss with whole group ways of representing houses with construction materials, encouraging broad and creative interpretations. Emphasize need to estimate size, model appropriate language; refer to last week's lessons on size Ensure children have appropriate choice of resources, according to ability. Provide opportunity for them to explore materials and experiment with ideas Adult support, ensuring all children are involved and have opportunities to discuss, listen and talk about their models. Take opportunity to model use of appropriate language, observe and assess children's developing spatial awareness and conceptual development	*Key language* English: Mathematical	*Resources* Large wooden bricks, large plastic bricks, small construction bricks (Lego)	*Whole class* *Group* 12 children 3–4 & 1/2 *Free choice*	Personal, Social and Emotional Language and Literacy *Mathematics* Knowledge and Understanding Physical Creative

Evaluation

As the activity was being video-taped, this will help me assess if all my learning intentions were being met. I felt as I circulated around the groups that the children were involved in the task. Some groups were having a group discussion, whereas others were working individually but still creating a house from them. There were also some children crossing over to other groups. These children were the ones involved in working with large construction bricks. They were also being very creative with the bricks, making them become a variety of household effects.

One lovely example of the children's play was when the children working with the wooden bricks had a window collapse while one of the children was in bed. Another explained how they had got her out and too much glass had gone on her. Then another child arrived from across the room as the council man to assess the change; originally this child had been helping some others construct a building with some different bricks. This helped my practitioner's intent that children learn in small and large groups.

VIDEO – ENTITLEMENT 6

(a) The Hedgehog and (b) Blast Off

Young children are entitled to engage in individual and dynamic play and learning experiences relevant to their age and development

These last two cameos illustrate the dynamic nature of play. The first, The Hedgehog, is a very structured setting, whereas 'Blast Off' was spontaneously initiated by the children and captured by a passing cameraman.

The Hedgehog

In the first cameo, the adult role is critical in ensuring the learning intention is reflected in children's play. Claire introduces the lesson by recalling the previous day's activities, encouraging the children to review, assess and modify their models in the light of yesterday's experiences. She reminds them of some of the problems they encountered.

Today they are making vehicles for the toys. Claire encourages the children to solve problems, sometimes through questioning or assisting them. She encourages them to articulate the processes of model-making, then, when sure they are able to work independently or with support from each other, she moves away. Her understanding of their levels of competence enables her to say, 'I bet you can fix the wheels yourself'. Then she moves on. She encourages and engages in the excitement and discovery of their success, 'Look, she's done it!' A celebration of the work concludes the lesson, leaving the Hedgehog securely sealed in his box.

Working across the headings of StEPs helps to assess the learning and plan for future learning. In column A of Entitlement 6, in the **Intellectual** row, we read that children are able to qualify their own likes and dislikes; they are spontaneous, responsive, become absorbed and 'own' tasks. Under column C, we read that children need to learn how

Claire's learning plan

Activity	Hedgehog
Area of curriculum	Technology
Organization	Choice – from a range of resources in creative and construction area
Development	Intellectual
Learning goals	*Select the materials* they need to construct vehicle for toys children have brought in from home; *make decision, assemble* and *join securely* the materials they have chosen
Principle	Young children are entitled to engage in individual and dynamic play and learning experiences relevant to their age and development
Resources	Construction, range of materials to join together
Activity	Review yesterday's lesson in which vehicles were made from children's toys. Discuss some of the methods used, identify the issues. Do children want to make any modifications? Does it need to be stronger? Faster? Bigger? More secure? Encourage children to share suggestions and solve problems
Evaluation	Children used a range of previously learned techniques, displayed knowledge of the properties of materials used and how different resources might fit together. They created their own ideas, adapting where necessary. They were working well together – helping each other, appropriate use of language
Adult role	Use children's ideas to encourage problem-solving

to respond to others' ideas and questions; to listen actively; to judge and estimate distance, direction and height; how to share ideas, experiences and interests.

> TO THINK ABOUT...
> Discuss how effectively these aspects have been achieved in this play activity.

Blast off!

The final cameo, 'Blast Off', also illustrates children engaged in individual and dynamic play and learning experiences relevant to their age and development. The adult has created an environment in which children work playfully within the framework of the curriculum. They have taken the space theme outside into their role play. Listen to the ways in which Debbie accepts the theme of their play while also extending and encouraging imaginative responses: 'Finish it off – you can't go to space until it's finished!' Debbie's questioning encourages the children to question each other: 'How can people fit in there?' Debbie captures the seriousness of their comment 'There's no more bricks!' by restating and reflecting their consternation, 'What can we do if there's no more bricks?' Yet she continues to encourage the children to resolve these issues.

This group of children are ready for their space adventure, while around their space capsule others are playing, collaboratively and independently on bikes and trikes, their play structured by the resources made available to them.

This was a spontaneous activity, initiated by the children from the earlier Space theme, so there is no independent plan for this activity. The general plan is shown earlier under Cameo 1.

> TO THINK ABOUT...
> Use StEPs to identify the aspects of pedagogical knowledge which have informed Debbie's responses. How has she challenged children, helped to sustain their play, adhered to the evidence before her of their own 'agenda', yet also provided opportunities for spontaneous, dynamic play?

FINALE

The cameos have illustrated different aspects of the Entitlements within elements of the curriculum. Reducing each cameo to 4/5 minutes has offered the opportunity for in-depth study of aspects of practice. However, inevitably this also means that many valuable aspects have been edited. The more formal structured sessions, literacy, guided reading, writing, numeracy, sometimes through use of ICT, all have a place in the curriculum. However, the purpose of the video has been to show you some ways in which children's learning and curriculum experiences may be enriched specifically through play with the engagement of other children and adults.

SECTION FIVE

The Statements of Entitlement to Play: explanation and charts

The aims of this section are to:
- Show what aspects are covered within the six Entitlements through the charts, which are reproduced at the end of the section.
- Talk you through the six Entitlements in general, giving examples through cameos and stories of what they look like in practice.

In Section 2, several of the practitioner-researchers expressed their surprise and frustration at how difficult it was at first to talk about beliefs and values and about teaching, learning and play, especially when challenged. The process of challenge, questioning individual beliefs and questioning each other was very demanding – at times, even painful! We experienced a process of deconstruction, taking apart all we believed in and then putting it under a microscope. We interrogated every phrase, every word. We were surprised at how many values we said we had and how many we did not really understand in any depth.

Once we had deconstructed our stated values and principles, we set about reading, exploring, talking, questioning, deliberating, redefining and reconstructing all the statements we had made at the beginning of the project. To further our own professional development and our work with children, we needed a set of statements that:

- would ensure our practice was underpinned by the knowledge we had rediscovered and acquired;
- were meaningful and accessible;
- would inform our planning and interactions with children in a way that would ensure we could provide a curriculum based on play.

The result was the StEPs, which represent the entire pedagogical process at a glance, evidence of which you may now already have seen on the video (Section 4) and read about in the Introduction.

Understanding more about how children learn and having a framework has changed the way the practitioner-researchers teach. We plan for opportunities to observe children at play and are better able to interpret what we see and hear. The evidence from those observations informs our planning. Placing all the information about teaching and learning in chart format has resulted in the information being readily accessible. We are able to ensure that principles inform practice. This really has made a difference to practice. Through StEPs, we are now able to teach and to advocate teaching in ways that are developmentally appropriate. *We are not bounded by the current curriculum frameworks yet are able to fulfil their expectations.*

The following charts show the Entitlements within the framework laid out in Figure 1.1 (Section 1). The columns can be read from top to bottom or side to side. The other strength of the charts is that you can add to them as you discover further relevant things about your children, setting or practitioners. To this end, we have also offered you blank charts for your own ideas. We hope you will want to invent new entitlements as you become familiar with this way of thinking, working and playing.

THE STATEMENTS OF ENTITLEMENT TO PLAY: EXPLANATION AND CHARTS

(1) Young children are entitled to play experiences that engage them affectively and socially in their own and others' learning

Column A From their development and prior learning, children are likely to know about:	Column B Development issue	Column C Children need to learn:	Column D From their professional knowledge and understanding, practitioners will know about:	Column E Practitioners will make provision for:	Column F Practitioners should teach:
• various social/cultural situations	social	• about different cultural/ethnic backgrounds • how to apply appropriate social conventions	• about different cultures • how to provide children with a positive self-image	• a learning environment that respects children's cultures and beliefs	• that all stereotypical roles can be challenged • appropriate skills in all children • by identifying children with special educational needs (SEN) and by acting as a role model
• their own gender		• positive sense of own gender • about gender through interaction	• that children will become gender-conscious and explore gender • about possible gender biases in play	• children to learn in a range of different contexts, with other children and adults • appropriate resources	• by ensuring access to development of activities, regardless of gender, ability, culture and ethnicity, through observation and evaluation • that stereotypical roles can be challenged • how to use/organize resources
• working as part of a group/individually		• to operate within a group • to be sensitive to the needs and feelings of others • to develop mature friendships • to share • a sense of fair play	• about children's social development • about group dynamics	• children to work within different groupings and individually	• esteem and respect for others
• confidence, security, acceptance (self and others)		• to develop sophisticated social skills in a variety of contexts • to build on trust and security in relationships • self-respect	• how to create a consistent but challenging framework	• consistency and continuity to allow children to work within different groupings and individually	• agreed values and codes of behaviour • through reassurance by giving and requiring explanations

| Column A
From their development and prior learning, children are likely to know about: | Column B
Development issue | Column C
Children need to learn: | Column D
From their professional knowledge and understanding, practitioners will know about: | Column E
Practitioners will make provision for: | Column F
Practitioners should teach: |
|---|---|---|---|---|---|
| • their own personal needs and an awareness of limitations of self and others

• taking risks and personal safety

• awareness of space and surroundings | physical | • about own personal needs
• limitations of self and others

• appropriate physical action and contact
• independence and self-help skills
• to extend physical capabilities with due regard to themselves and others
• about space and surroundings
• new and secure contexts | • how children develop an understanding of appropriate physical boundaries

• about health, safety and welfare issues | • a developmentally appropriate curriculum so that children can function independently or with assistance from peers and adults

• a safe and secure environment
• recording of evidence about children's welfare | • rules for socially and physically acceptable behaviour

• how to implement health and safety rules |
| • empowerment
• respect
• value systems
• acceptable/ unacceptable behaviours

• decision-making
• initiation of ideas
• setting parameters

• listening | intellectual | • to understand different perspectives and points of view
• the difference between right and wrong
• to adhere to acceptable types of behaviour, understanding consequences of actions
• to choose
• to be confident in worth of own ideas
• how to select and use resources independently
• the consequence of their actions
• persistence
• listening skills in different social contexts | • how to extend social play through posing problems
• how to intervene and structure learning

• the stages of development in children's learning and thinking
• about the backgrounds of children
• how children react in social situations
• about the need for ownership | • appropriate resources
• time for children to engage in trial-and-error play

• involving outside agencies to inform understanding of children within the wider cultural context
• work in partnership with other relevant professionals
• partnership with other professionals, staff and community | • by supporting children in their use of resources, for learning
• how to make choices
• about the consequences of their actions
• independent thinking

• understanding of others |

THE STATEMENTS OF ENTITLEMENT TO PLAY: EXPLANATION AND CHARTS

Column A From their development and prior learning, children are likely to know about:	Column B Development issue	Column C Children need to learn:	Column D From their professional knowledge and understanding, practitioners will know:	Column E Practitioners will make provision for:	Column F Practitioners should teach:
• positive relationship with peers and adults • having a sense of belonging • a supportive environment • prior emotional experiences • equilibrium • their own feelings	emotional	• about enjoying and needing companionship • to be enthusiastic about learning • to contribute to discussions • to ask questions • to make independent decisions about what is right or wrong • to explore feelings • to be responsive to their own feelings and those of others, including guilt and shame • to exercise self-control • to show a sense of humour	• how to develop positive responses with children • how to evaluate intentions/ objectives in a positive way • how to interpret emotional behaviours presented by children	• displays, assessment and evaluation procedures that support, reflect and celebrate young children's achievements • classroom to be organized to support and reflect a developmentally appropriate curriculum • time to observe behaviour and relationships • ongoing training for early years staff • partnership with other professionals	• how to evaluate positive role models • independence and responsibility for children's personal needs • use of appropriate language for expressing intentions and emotions • how to explore and express feelings • strategies for dealing with intense feelings
• verbalizing feelings and opinions • expressing thoughts and ideas • assertiveness	linguistic	• listening skills • questioning skills • to talk about experiences • to develop non-verbal communication skills and articulation • to engage in discussion • to use appropriate language for different audiences • appropriate expression of views and appreciation of others	• how to interpret children's talk • the processes of children becoming language users • how social relationships affect language use	• stimulating a desire to talk, listen and express ideas	• relevant, new vocabulary • communication skills • how and when to express views • that languages are used in different ways for different purposes and audiences • how to communicate through mark-making and writing

(2) Young children are entitled to play experiences that are set in meaningful and relevant activities and contexts for learning

Column A From their development and prior learning, children are likely to know about:	Column B Development issue	Column C Children need to learn:	Column D From their professional knowledge and understanding, practitioners will know:	Column E Practitioners will make provision for:	Column F Practitioners should teach:
• links with home and school • responsibility for selves, others and the environment • making relationships	social	• to share life experiences • to respond to living things with care and concern • to be trusted and to trust others • to be respected and to respect others • about the complexities of roles and responsibilities	• what is meaningful and relevant in children's lives • about the influence of home on children's education • how to acknowledge and respect cultural and ethnic diversity • the influence of socio-dramatic play on children's social learning • how to motivate the children to use prior knowledge and to aid learning	• a learning environment that reflects children's starting points, their families and features of the area and community in which they live • socio-dramatic play	• temporal events in their lives • different forms of interaction • what it means to show respect • empathy/ sympathy towards others • how to be fair and equitable • care of self and others
• using familiar equipment and extension of skills • awareness of personal needs and limitations • their bodies	physical	• confidence, in their own ability with familiar equipment • to extend fine and gross motor skills	• developmental differences and the effect of prior experience on physical competence and confidence • how to provide a secure stimulating environment	• different levels of physical challenge • a safe environment to allow children to test their physical skills • promoting independence and confidence • different levels of ability • the extension of fine and gross motor skills	• implications of body language • different forms of physical expression • quality in movement skills • appropriate behaviour and safety rules in the indoor/outdoor context • how to access and be responsible for a range of resources

THE STATEMENTS OF ENTITLEMENT TO PLAY: EXPLANATION AND CHARTS

| Column A
From their development and prior learning, children are likely to know about: | Column B
Development issue | Column C
Children need to learn: | Column D
From their professional knowledge and understanding, practitioners will know: | Column E
Practitioners will make provision for: | Column F
Practitioners should teach: |
|---|---|---|---|---|---|
| • understanding others' perspective
• contributing their own prior experiences and knowledge

• the world around them
• the concepts of time, numbers, print, shapes, size, etc. | intellectual | • metacognitive skills
• perseverance
• concentration

• classification and discriminatory skills
• memorization strategies
• memorization skills
• to reflect
• to set their own targets
• to make use of previous experiences
• to be learners
• to be curious
• about the passing of time – past, present, future
• to refine and develop mathematical, scientific, technological, historical, geographical, musical and creative concepts | • how to motivate

• how to plan a broad, balanced and relevant curriculum
• how to relate children's abilities and interests to the learning context
• about all-round child development and skill transference
• children's learning and metacognition
• children's conceptual development
• the use of target setting for differentiating learning experiences | • differentiated group and individual activities

• building on children's prior knowledge

• children's reflection on their own learning needs | • concepts of past, present and future
• meta-cognitive strategies
• simple targeting skills
• how to identify stereotyped images
• that boys and girls can achieve equally |
| • self-esteem through having prior experience valued
• a personal sense of worth and of valuing prior experience
• how their behaviour may affect the feelings of others | emotional | • to trust and value themselves, their own thoughts and actions
• to self-evaluate
• autonomy and self-reliance
• how to accept correction, support and praise
• show consideration towards living things | • how to recognize and enhance attitudes
• how to provide security
• about scaffolding individual learning and development
• about child development | • purposeful structures within classroom organization that promote independence
• familiar yet challenging experiences that build on children's strengths
• intervening in children's play
• a balance of the curriculum with children's developmental needs | • respectful and enquiring attitudes to similarities and differences |

| Column A
From their development and prior learning, children are likely to know about: | Column B
Development issue | Column C
Children need to learn: | Column D
From their professional knowledge and understanding, practitioners will know about: | Column E
Practitioners will make provision for: | Column F
Practitioners should teach: |
|---|---|---|---|---|---|
| • role playing and improvising | emotional cont. | • to be spontaneous and flexible
• to reflect | • how to interpret behaviour
• how to promote self-esteem | • contexts for learning that build on children's prior knowledge and learning
• promoting children's self-esteem by valuing their contributions | |
| • the need to listen and respond appropriately

• their own home and family language

• vocabulary, sentence and grammatical structure

• playing with words and having fun with language | linguistic | • listening skills, oral skills, discriminatory skills
• questioning and responding skills
• to become confident speakers
• that language is dynamic
• the diversity of language
• to talk about their own life experiences
• to talk with increasing vocabulary and grammatical structure
• genres within languages, e.g. delighting in inventing jokes
• literacy skills, e.g. rhyme, rhythm, metre | • about verbal and non-verbal communication
• how cultural and environmental experiences affect literacy and oracy

• how children become literate
• how to use and extend home language | • opportunities for children to talk with each other and with adults
• children to communicate in their home language

• access to a range of text, illustrations and environmental print
• a wide range of children's mark-making | • questioning and answering skills
• skills of rhyming, sequencing
• (provide for) talking and listening in home languages
• the use of language appropriate to context
• new vocabulary, specific to contexts
• how to share experiences and listen to or value the experiences of others
• children's involvement in culturally diverse genre: poetry, rhymes, songs and stories |

THE STATEMENTS OF ENTITLEMENT TO PLAY: EXPLANATION AND CHARTS

(3) Young children are entitled to play experiences that promote curiosity and the use of imagination and creativity in learning

Column A From their development and prior learning, children are likely to know about:	Column B Development issue	Column C Children need to learn:	Column D From their professional knowledge and understanding, practitioners will know about:	Column E Practitioners will make provision for:	Column F Practitioners should teach:
• learning in a social context • interaction • elaborate play with objects	social	• to reason with others • to negotiate and cooperate • to include others in events • to take turns • to explore and respond to sensory experiences	• the ways in which children express feelings • the cultural and ethnic background of the children • family background	• opportunities for children to initiate ideas within groups • partnership within families and communities • interaction with others in previous/present settings • developing a sense of ownership of the environment by the children	• how to initiate and respond to ideas • use of imagination in play and talk • through extending and widening opportunities
• using a range of familiar/unfamiliar materials/equipment	physical	• to handle tools and materials with increased control and coordination • to apply such skills with imagination and creativity	• a range of activities/media that will challenge and stimulate all children • generating confidence and trust • child development in order to extend their skills • extending physical experimentation to prepare for imaginative/creative development	• a wide range of resources to stimulate and challenge	• appropriate use of tools and resources
• learning concepts by enactment, role taking • sound, colour, texture, shape, form, space in 2D and 3D	intellectual	• to compare and contrast fantasy and reality • to sustain a situation/ability to stay in role • to reflect • to cope with abstract symbols • to solve problems	• valuing and promoting imagination • children needing to learn to think symbolically	• imaginative areas/displays	• children to be confident with imaginative play/creativity by challenging stereotypes • a range of skills using a wide variety of tools and materials

Column A From their development and prior learning, children are likely to know about:	Column B Development issue	Column C Children need to learn:	Column D From their professional knowledge and understanding, practitioners will know about:	Column E Practitioners will make provision for:	Column F Practitioners should teach:
• rhythm and sound • ownership • individual interpretation • fantasy and reality • use of own ideas • humour	**intellectual cont.**	 • to initiate ideas • to laugh at oneself/situation, laughing with other people	• how to develop abstract representation • being accepted as part of imaginative play by the children • the process of creative learning • not reducing everything to skills	• expression through choice and a variety of resources • establishing trust among all learners (children and adults) • exploratory play • valuing the processes of learning	• how to form an imaginative response to creative stimuli, e.g. music, artefacts • supporting and modelling creative and imaginative play • children to collaborate and play alongside peers and adults • skills and provide opportunities for children to make their own inventive responses to stimuli • by valuing the children's own responses
• exploration of feelings in a supportive environment • unself-conscious play • self-image • experiencing different environments • celebrating success and making mistakes	**emotional**	• how to communicate feelings • how to cope with different feelings • to respond to a range of stimuli such as art, music and drama • to adapt to challenge and change • to not fear failure • to trust self and others • to take risks with ideas	• promoting positive self-awareness • objectively interpreting children's behaviours and emotional responses • children needing to explore and express a range of emotions through imagination/ creativity	• a positive ethos within the learning environment that respects individual differences • offering support through sensitive use of language and gestures • time to offer skilful intervention • feeling safe and secure in a familiar environment	• an awareness of other people's feelings • knowledge and skills for early citizenship • an awareness of other children's different needs and abilities • appropriate ways of expressing ideas and fantasies

THE STATEMENTS OF ENTITLEMENT TO PLAY: EXPLANATION AND CHARTS

| Column A
From their development and prior learning, children are likely to know about: | Column B
Development issue | Column C
Children need to learn: | Column D
From their professional knowledge and understanding, practitioners will know about: | Column E
Practitioners will make provision for: | Column F
Practitioners should teach: |
|---|---|---|---|---|---|
| • communicating ideas
• talking about their experiences

• describing events and objects | linguistic | • listening skills
• to role play
• to narrate and tell stories
• evaluation/ negotiation skills

• to talk about familiar and new experiences
• discipline and expressive vocabulary | • children's use of expressive, descriptive language
• awareness of non-verbal expressions
• the introduction of new vocabulary

• that linguistic skills are integral to all others, not a separate entity
• development of social linguistic patterns
• development of memorization
• the value of having fun with words | • differentiated reinforcement of vocabulary

• play contexts that promote language

• situations where talk is respected and vocabulary developed | • by extending vocabulary
• communication skills
• to reflect and imagine
• by providing for an increasingly developed vocabulary
• how to ask questions to satisfy one's curiosity

• rhymes, songs, experimentation with sounds and words |

(4) Young children are entitled to engage in play experiences that are open-ended and offer trial-and-error learning without fear of failure

Column A From their development and prior learning, children are likely to know about:	Column B Development issue	Column C Children need to learn:	Column D From their professional knowledge and understanding, practitioners will know about:	Column E Practitioners will make provision for:	Column F Practitioners should teach:
• working individually • interaction • communication	social	• to listen to others • to cooperate • to collaborate • to conform • how to participate in small social groups	• how to support children's development as problem solvers and risk takers	• adults to act as role models • relevant ways in which children's efforts can be celebrated	• flexibility, risk taking • respect for the opinions of others • the sharing of ideas through observations, asking questions, exploring, making choices
• being interested in their environment		• to concentrate, persevere	• that children will become gender-conscious and explore gender • how to provide children with a positive self-image	• non-stereotypical resources including people • opportunities when child's family can enhance the learning • rewarding and correcting children's efforts and achievements	• through challenging stereotypes to ensure access to development of activities, regardless of gender
• flexibility • self-awareness		• to make choices • to recognize own and others' ideas	• how to create a consistent fair and inclusive framework	• flexibility within a framework • successful interactions with others	
• competence with equipment • their own bodies	physical	• responsibility in use of tools, equipment, materials • coordination, balance/agility	• about health and safety issues	• a safe and secure environment • involving outside agencies when necessary • an environment that promotes child development	• how to be safe • understanding and appreciation of health and safety rules
• challenging their own physical boundaries		• how to extend their capabilities	• what resources are appropriate for holistic development through play	• a wide range of resources, made of different man-made and natural resources	• through use of resources that promote fine and gross motor development

THE STATEMENTS OF ENTITLEMENT TO PLAY: EXPLANATION AND CHARTS

| Column A
From their development and prior learning, children are likely to know about: | Column B
Development issue | Column C
Children need to learn: | Column D
From their professional knowledge and understanding, practitioners will know about: | Column E
Practitioners will make provision for: | Column F
Practitioners should teach: |
|---|---|---|---|---|---|
| • knowledge of objects/materials | intellectual | • to see differences and similarities
• to recognize patterns | • what resources are appropriate to support children's learning
• how to extend social play through posing problems | • a range of resources to support conceptual and curriculum development
• imaginative/role play opportunities | • motivation and increased concentration
• and challenge through experimentation with new materials |
| • knowledge of immediate environment
• consolidation of present knowledge
• extension of existing knowledge
• initiation of ideas | | • spatial awareness
• to consolidate and extend their knowledge of the world
• to evaluate and re-evaluate
• to estimate and make credible guesses | | • a stimulating and challenging environment that supports children to develop understanding of the world around them
• appropriate resources that will challenge learning, within Zone of Proximal Development | • mathematical and scientific concepts
• how to formulate plans and strategies
• information retrieval |
| • recognition of a problem
• asking questions

• needing help | | • to hypothesize
• to be able to formulate questions
• to restructure ideas and solve problems
• to order and make comparisons
• to develop psychomotor skills
• to seek help from adults, peers and community | • how to intervene and structure learning | • time for children to plan their own learning
• taking child's ideas on board
• keeping work so that it can be re-presented later | |

| Column A
From their development and prior learning, children are likely to know about: | Column B
Development issue | Column C
Children need to learn: | Column D
From their professional knowledge and understanding, practitioners will know about: | Column E
Practitioners will make provision for: | Column F
Practitioners should teach: |
|---|---|---|---|---|---|
| • self-esteem

• challenge, risk taking, coping and competition
• their place in the world | **emotional** | • to be self-motivated
• to persevere

• to be confident about experimenting
• to be comfortable about success and failure or partially solving a situation
• to cope with not knowing
• to overcome anxieties
• that their own ideas are valued | • the influence of role models on children's attitudes and dispositions for learning
• how to develop positive models with children
• how to interpret
• emotional problems/ behaviours presented by children | • times when words associated with feelings and relationships can be explored

• sensitive ways of dealing with emotional problems/ behaviours – known to all other relevant adults
• sensory, hands-on activities, use of environment in widest sense | • an appreciation of the feelings of others
• that failure is acceptable
• strategies for dealing with feelings
• the use of language to explore and express feelings |
| • verbalizing own experiences
• communication
• acquiring new language

• mark-making | **linguistic** | • to use language to communicate and verbalize own experiences
• to convey meanings and ideas
• to listen
• to question
• to articulate
• to make marks and record ideas | • how to interpret children's understanding from their language
• the importance of language in the development of their conceptual understanding
• how social relationships affect language use | • time to listen

• the introduction and modelling and use of new language
• large and small discussion groups | • ways of expressing their understanding
• relevant vocabulary
• how to participate in discussions |

(5) Young children are entitled to playful, exploratory and experiential activities with a variety of materials and resources and within a variety of contexts

| Column A
From their development and prior learning, children are likely to know about: | Column B
Development issue | Column C
Children need to learn: | Column D
From their professional knowledge and understanding, practitioners will know about: | Column E
Practitioners will make provision for: | Column F
Practitioners should teach: |
|---|---|---|---|---|---|
| • making responses in various contexts
• playing in a range of social contexts
• playing individually and as part of a group | social | • how to respond appropriately in different social contexts
• to operate as an individual and within a group
• to make discoveries, individually and collaboratively with or without an adult
• that each child has equal entitlement to these activities | • different cultures
• acting as a role model
• creating a consistent framework
• children becoming gender-conscious
• how to address potential biases and inequalities | • all children to engage in activities
• challenging stereotypes
• consistent routines
• access to activities, regardless of gender
• different social contexts for learning | • how to provide children with a positive self-image
• appropriate use of resources, materials and tools
• how to select an activity
• how to use and explore materials
• how to learn in small and large groups |
| • finding out for themselves
• sensory experience
• taking risks
• personal safety | physical | • visual and auditory skills
• through using all their senses
• restraint and control of actions
• appropriate physical action and contact
• how to handle tools safely with increasing expertise | • health and safety issues
• psychomotor development | • appropriate and accessible resources
• safety within the learning environment
• a range of resources to promote fine and gross motor skills | • and implement health/safety rules
• appropriate use of resources and tools |

| Column A
From their development and prior learning, children are likely to know about: | Column B
Development issue | Column C
Children need to learn: | Column D
From their professional knowledge and understanding, practitioners will know about: | Column E
Practitioners will make provision for: | Column F
Practitioners should teach: |
|---|---|---|---|---|---|
| • interacting with materials and resources in a range of contexts
• using sensory experiences to investigate their world
• properties of materials
• cause and effect
• combining materials to make something new or different
• concentration
• asking questions | intellectual | • to distinguish different characteristics of properties of materials
• to classify, generalize and discriminate
• to ask questions such as 'why . . . ?' and 'what if . . . ?'
• to hypothesize, evaluate, make decisions, recall
• to sustain ideas
• meta-cognition
• discrimination and memory | • the need to develop positive responses with children
• how to communicate intentions/ objectives in a positive way | • appropriate resources
• opportunities for children to take risks with their ideas
• resources that encourage responses | • assertive discipline
• self-discipline and self-management
• the value of making contributions
• the importance of being open to new experiences
• use of language
• role model |
| • differentiating between positive and negative experiences
• developing a sense of self
• being curious

• the need to follow basic hygiene customs | emotional | • to express responses appropriately
• to state preferences and make independent decisions
• to develop care of self with increasing reliability and care
• to be open to new experiences
• perseverance
• to develop care of self with increasing reliability and independence | • the need to develop positive responses with children | • appropriate resources for engaging emotional responses
• opportunities for children to take risks with their ideas
• resources that encourage emotional/feelings responses | • assertive discipline strategies
• self-discipline and self-management
• the value of making contributions
• the importance of being open to new experiences |
| • different types of language for different purposes and a range of experiences
• communicating or describing their discoveries | linguistic | • appropriate language to express familiar and new experiences
• cultural procedures for talking to different people in different contexts
• to label materials and resources | • how language is used to formulate ideas and describe discoveries
• how different contexts and purposes affect language use | • a language-rich, stimulating environment that motivates articulation of ideas
• learning and new technical language | • the skills necessary to become language users
• extending linguistic structures
• descriptive techniques, e.g. more complex structure, use of adjectives and new vocabulary |

(6) Young children are entitled to engage in individual and dynamic play and learning experiences relevant to their age group and stage of development

| Column A
From their development and prior learning, children are likely to know about: | Column B
Development issue | Column C
Children need to learn: | Column D
From their professional knowledge and understanding, practitioners will know about: | Column E
Practitioners will make provision for: | Column F
Practitioners should teach: |
|---|---|---|---|---|---|
| • how to pretend and what is real
• having and making friends
• different social forms of play, e.g. playing alone, playing alongside others
• their own place in the family hierarchy
• gaining attention | social | • to explore and challenge different roles
• to adapt to different social roles and rules
• to conform to others' expectations in a wide sphere of people
• how to pretend with others and accept and value their contribution
• other acceptable ways of gaining attention
• to seek help when needed from adults, peers and resources
• further skills in cooperating and collaborating with adults and peers
• about their own place in the wider hierarchy and in relation to others | • the social context of learning (15) (Pollard)
• the importance of friendships and friendship groupings
• social forms of play | • a wide range of social contexts for learning
• being a co-player
• modelling playful behaviour
• children to function in pairs and small/large groups
• observing individual and groups of children | • group skills and group ethics
• how to defer gratification
• turn-taking |
| • use of space
• own current gross and fine motor abilities
• different environments for using physical skills
• some of their own physical strengths and bodily limitations
• the kinds of physical activity that they enjoy | physical | • the importance of personal, individual space for self and others
• how to extend current physical capabilities
• to adapt to different physical environments
• greater control over own gross motor skills
• to handle objects with greater precision
• about their own physical strength and its effects | • stages of physical development in children from birth to 8 years
• the importance of personal space for children
• the range of children's likely responses to physical challenge | • opportunities to observe and interpret children's physical responses
• supporting and extending relationships
• a range of different tools and media to extend children's capabilities | • spatial awareness and distance
• how to handle a wide range of tools capably
• a wider range of physical capabilities and skills
• about body capabilities |

| Column A
From their development and prior learning, children are likely to know about: | Column B
Development issue | Column C
Children need to learn: | Column D
From their professional knowledge and understanding, practitioners will know about: | Column E
Practitioners will make provision for: | Column F
Practitioners should teach: |
|---|---|---|---|---|---|
| • the things they are good at and the things they are not so good at
• how to qualify their own likes and dislikes
• being spontaneous, responsive and immediate
• how to become absorbed and 'own' a task
• routines and sequences in their daily lives
• own family values and morality
• making personal choices
• assuming different characters in role play | intellectual | • respect for other viewpoints and ideas
• how to handle and appreciate others' viewpoints
• to make own appropriate responses
• to wait for others to make their responses
• how to respond to others' ideas and questions
• how to listen actively
• how to observe and notice similarities and differences and to differentiate
• to judge and estimate distance, direction and height
• wider moral values
• how to share ideas, experiences and interests | • cognitive development and constructivism
• scaffolding and its role in developing children's individual learning
• recent brain studies research and its growing contribution to understanding of learning processes
• knowledge of curriculum content and how each aspect is best learned and taught
• how children generate and respond to different types of questions
• how children of this age react to moral dilemmas | • understanding of how individual children are likely to approach different tasks/ activities
• the current level of each child's understanding within curriculum aspects
• challenging individual children's existing knowledge and skills
• validating children's play and choice
• children to extend and consolidate skills and concepts
• 'comfortable challenge' (Merry 1998)
• purposeful learning activities that meet individual needs and choice making | • comparative skills
• observation techniques and skills
• listening skills through offering something worthwhile to listen to
• estimation
• how to raise, and respond to, questions in a variety of ways
• through provision of direct, first-hand experiences
• how to form and express opinions relating to task |
| • expressing a range of feelings
• responding to others' expression of feelings
• centrality of self
• feelings of enjoyment and fun | emotional | • the effect of making different choices
• wider moral values
• deferred gratification
• emotional security through being valued and respected | • children's likely responses to different emotions
• how children acquire emotional security
• handling children with a range of emotional problems
• behaviour modification strategies
• different moralities | • learning about how each child feels about her or himself
• observing, analysing and interpreting children's behaviours
• an environment that promotes and supports individual children's spiritual, moral, social and cultural development
• acknowledging children's | • the meaning behind different cultural and religious events and beliefs
• how to voice personal concerns rationally
• the formation and acceptance of opinions
• techniques for individual expression of ideas
• an appreciation of deferred gratification |

THE STATEMENTS OF ENTITLEMENT TO PLAY: EXPLANATION AND CHARTS

Column A From their development and prior learning, children are likely to know about:	Column B Development issue	Column C Children need to learn:	Column D From their professional knowledge and understanding, practitioners will know about:	Column E Practitioners will make provision for:	Column F Practitioners should teach:
				emotional responses and learning • sustaining and raising children's self-esteem	• ways of expressing and evaluating their feelings, making responses and choices
• stating likes and dislikes • assuming different character voices in role play • how to talk appropriately within a small circle of acquaintances • verbal and non-verbal communication • recognizing familiar voices and noises • the functions of language and words	linguistic	• vocabulary for expressing personal concerns and needs • wider functions and use of language in educational context • the language of the educational community • reasoning with and through language • to construct and re-construct stories and characters	• different forms and functions of language • likely stages in oracy and literacy development • how children acquire a sense of audience • the role of communication in socio-dramatic play	• correct modelling of linguistic behaviours • interacting with and extending children's speech	• how to use different language in different contexts • storying skills and characterization • vocabulary relevant to particular play and learning contexts • new vocabulary • functions and uses of language • how language affects other people's responses • oracy and literacy skills • by talking, reading and writing as a model

Blank chart for your own use

| Column A
From their development and prior learning, children are likely to know about: | Column B
Development issue | Column C
Children need to learn: | Column D
From their professional knowledge and understanding, practitioners will know about: | Column E
Practitioners will make provision for: | Column F
Practitioners should teach: |
|---|---|---|---|---|---|
| | social | | | | |
| | physical | | | | |
| | intellectual | | | | |
| | emotional | | | | |
| | linguistic | | | | |

SECTION SIX

StEPs and curricular links

The aims of this section are to:
- Outline the strong links between StEPs, Foundation Stage Guidance and Curriculum 2000 for KS1.
- Indicate the rationale (reasoning) behind each Entitlement.
- Show how StEPs actually operates in practice through a series of cameos linked to each of the six Entitlements.
- Emphasize within the cameo stories the role of the **adults** in supporting children in a StEPs framework.
- Explain the detailed charts for all six Entitlements.

Most curriculum documents set out in detail a number of aims or principles against which a particular curriculum framework should be used. The Foundation Stage Guidance and Key Stage One (KS1) of the National Curriculum (NC) are two such documents. The former is non-statutory while the latter is a statutory requirement. All statutory documents require action in law, whereas non-statutory materials are deemed to be 'recommendations' as in the case of most foundation stage curricula. Similar documents exist in many other countries (e.g. Norway 1994; SED 1995 & 1999; OHMCI 1998; Welsh Office 1998) and readers outside England should establish the requirement basis of their own curriculum documentation.

We have used the Foundation Stage and KS1 as the basis of our Pack because this is the context for the practitioner-researchers who have developed these materials. However, StEPs embraces principles from other curricula documents and can, therefore, be used in other contexts.

The first principle presented in the Foundation Stage Guidance states that 'Effective education requires both a relevant curriculum and practitioners who understand and are able to implement the curriculum requirements' (QCA 2000a: 3). StEPs enable practitioners to make informed decisions and to promote the relevance of activities and context so that they can understand and implement the curriculum. Section 8, the Child Development Charts, is a starting point for analysing the stage of development that each child has reached and to then match the curriculum to the child's current level.

The Foundation Stage Guidance presents a fourth principle: 'Early years experience should build on what children already know and can do' (p. 11). Each of the Entitlements starts from the premise that the *prior learning* the child brings on entering any particular provision or setting is the soundest basis from which to begin teaching and implementing an appropriate curriculum. StEPs encourages practitioners to gain information about the children from parents and other sources and to select relevant elements through which to advance children's experiences. The way the Entitlements are presented in chart form means that key aspect can readily be identified and children's developmental needs tracked.

The fifth and seventh principles of the Foundation Stage Guidance state: 'No child should be excluded or disadvantaged' and 'To be effective, an early years curriculum needs to be carefully structured' (p. 11). Through the Entitlements, each child's special and developmental needs can be pinpointed and supported to establish a way forward for that particular child. For example, within each Entitlement the first column (A) enables the practitioner to identify the child's personal needs and prior learning. The next two columns (B and C) help to target areas for development and the three practitioner-related columns (D, E and F) show examples of how to manage and provide for the child's learning from those starting points.

The underlying principle of the Entitlements is to give children opportunities to be engaged in purposeful and meaningful activities, partly through their own auspices and partly through experiences provided by the adults. The eleventh principle enshrined in the Foundation Stage Guidance suggests, 'For children to have rich and stimulating experiences, the learning environment should be well planned and well organized' (p. 12). For this to happen, children must be able to relate immediately to provision that they will understand, respect and value.

A key feature of the whole StEPs Pack is the role of the practitioner. The ninth principle of the Foundation Stage Guidance states that 'Practitioners must be able to observe and respond appropriately to children' (p. 11). While this may appear self-evident, it is often the case – as the practitioner-researchers discovered in analysing their practice – that settings can be run in ways that fit the interests of adults and make life run smoothly for them, which is not always the same thing as responding to what observations inform us about children's interests.

The practitioner's crucial role appears again in the tenth principle, which refers to 'well planned, purposeful activity and appropriate intervention by practitioners' (p. 11). Each Entitlement provides a pathway to help practitioners to formulate a route to further a child's learning, providing a scaffold for adults to plan learning and teaching opportunities.

According to the third principle of the Foundation Stage Guidance, 'practitioners need to ensure that all children feel included, secure and valued'. Above all else, the Entitlements are all-encompassing and place the child at the centre of all planned activities with specific consideration to the vital adult guidance, maintenance and care role. Use of StEPs ensures that 'parents and practitioners must work together' (principle 6, Foundation Stage Guidance, p. 11) in order for the knowledge that each has of the child to be embedded within the curriculum provided. It must be stressed at this point that interpretation of the Entitlements will depend on the setting's situation and ethos but the child's entitlements implicit within StEPs are non-negotiable.

In summary, the Foundation Stage Guidance document emphasizes that, above all, 'effective learning and development for young children requires high quality care and education by practitioners' (p. 12). It is the clear intention of StEPs to support practitioners to evaluate and improve their practice.

Users of this Pack will find, once they get used to the layout, that they can speedily cross-reference the aims of the Foundation Stage subsumed within the Foundation Stage Guidance with StEPs.

Within **KS1 of the National Curriculum** (DfEE 1999), the two main aims are:

- to provide opportunities for all pupils to learn and to achieve; and
- to promote pupils' spiritual, moral, social and cultural development and prepare all pupils for the opportunities, responsibilities and experiences of life.

What better way to do this than to start from children as individuals and the learning about the world that they have achieved through the family, the community and the early educational settings they have attended? Following the Foundation Stage, the child's developmental needs continue to extend and follow the same principles as underlined in StEPs. These can be utilized as a checklist and emphasize that the curriculum needs to be broad and balanced and to be age and ability appropriate. Hence the continuity of the Entitlements from the Foundation Stage through to the primary phase of education and beyond, for there is no doubt that these early experiences serve as a foundation for lifelong learning and development as learners.

Working with the ideas for StEPs, we all felt that we needed a 'cubic' model to describe the process of interrelating curriculum to entitlement to child development (Figure 6.1). It is important that practitioners don't try to operate a 'wish list' when they interpret the contents of StEPs. We found that it was easy to tick away happily at the various columns in the **hope** – rather than the **knowledge** – that these areas were 'covered' by the kinds of provision being made for learning. Through our

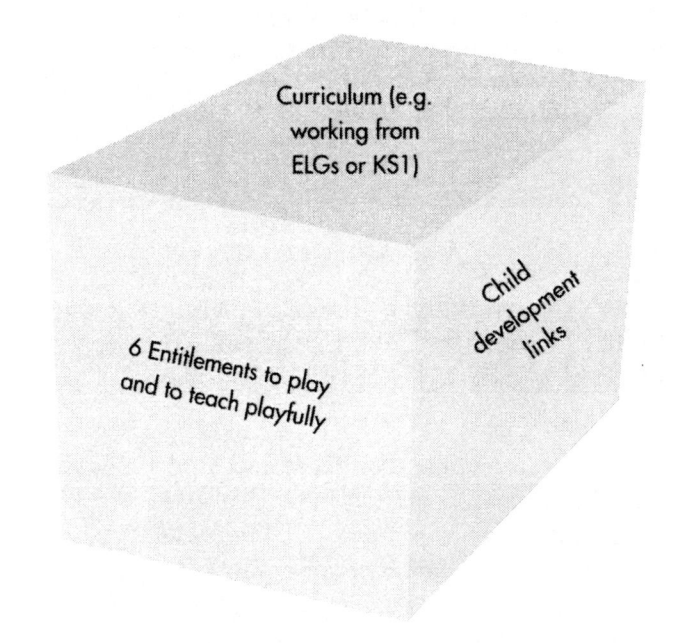

Figure 6.1 Cubic model of curriculum, entitlement and child development

intense discussions we recognized that, while we could suggest that every activity provided children with 'opportunities' and 'experiences', it was how we planned for and presented these that influenced the **real learning** outcomes. Providing a table full of jigsaws *may* offer children opportunities for understanding pattern and shape, but what evidence do we have that this is actually happening for these children at this jigsaw table on this day? Similarly, putting out interesting, colourful games intended to develop counting skills *may* inspire the children to play with them, but we still need **evidence** that our learning intentions have been met. This could mean playing alongside the children and posing challenges within your own 'game', as the following practitioner did:

Practitioner: Oh, I've thrown a 5 and a 3 on the dice – can I move seven spaces?
Chorus from Y1 children: No, it's 8, move 8, you've got to move 8!
Practitioner: I don't think so . . . look. (She counts the 5 pattern but deliberately misses the middle spot.)
Children: You missed the middle dot. You must count it again.
The practitioner counts again including all the spots and confirms that she has 8.

The children are pleased that, for once, they appeared to know more than the practitioner.

But think about what evidence the practitioner has about the children's secure knowledge of number bonds. Playing with children in this way frequently offers 'surprises' in terms of what they can know and do in situations where testing is not overt.

A WORD ABOUT PERSONAL SOCIAL & HEALTH EDUCATION (PSHE) AND CITIZENSHIP

With the Curriculum 2000 revisions (DfEE 1999), 'new' sections emerged to be included: those of PSHE and Citizenship. In KS1 – as we would argue in the Foundation Stage – these elements will not be taught as discrete 'subjects', but will be integrated into other curriculum activities to add breadth, enrichment and a more 'human' dimension, focusing as they do on children's *responses* to experiences and not just upon the *content* of those experiences. Children acquire a sense of citizenship by being taught the components of 'good citizenship' not simply by being told that they need to be good citizens, however phrased! These 'new' cross-curricular dimensions link well with all elements within the StEPs Pack, focusing as they do on rights, responsibilities and, yes, entitlements to certain kinds of experiences for learners and citizens.

We underestimate young children if we don't accept that they are capable of significant thought about issues such as citizenship and personal decision-making. One of the writers remembers vividly in her own nursery when sharing 2 pedal cars, 4 bikes and 3 scooters among 24 children was a real issue. No amount of asking children to 'take turns' or 'share' worked. In desperation, she sat down with the children and asked, 'What can we do to make sure everyone has a turn and that the situation is good for everyone?' To her delight the children came up with at least four ways in which a 'fair system' could be operated, one solution for which was that children on the vehicles should be allowed to go twice around the outdoor play area before having to relinquish the bike to the next person selected by the adult. Even this was eventually changed so that lists of names were written for those who wanted to play on individual vehicles and they were ticked off in turn (usually by a child). It was then discussed with the children why this was or was not a situation that was good for everyone. Young children can vote on issues of concern for them and this was one situation in which they were able to offer a vote on which system worked best to ensure parity for all.

ASSESSMENT – A 'GOLDEN THREAD' WITHIN THE CURRICULUM AND StEPs

We recognized early in our deliberations within the project that certain aspects of 'good' practice underpinned all others – our 'golden threads' – one of which was the assessment of children, often through observation. Within early years settings, assessment has become an on-going focus for practitioners, which, at best, helps to sharpen the support that is given to children of all abilities, differentiated according to need. The Pack itself operates on this basis – what you observe will need to be included within your knowledge base (Column D) as a basis for thinking about what else might be provided. (For those of you who would like to read more about assessment, there is a section within the Annotated Bibliography on this issue.)

On entry to school, it has become a statutory requirement that, within the first half-term of beginning Year 1, children are closely observed and assessments made within the areas of Language, Numeracy and Personal and Social development. Baseline Assessment Schemes are many and varied but all include these particular areas (see, for example, Birmingham City Council/NFER-Nelson 1997; QCA 1997). In support of these assessment schemes, many local authorities have produced guidance materials to help practitioners in making initial assessments of the children. The context of many such assessments is, of course, children's play (as the cameo below, and many others in this pack, exemplifies). Play is a naturalistic context for assessment: children can often show in their play competence and confidence, which may be hidden from observers in more formal situations. One example would be the 3-year-old who could name just about every garden bird both in 'the flesh' and in picture form, yet when presented with a line drawing of a duck (very different from the reality

StEPs AND CURRICULAR LINKS

or the photo form) shook his head in dismay rather than lack of knowledge!

Once made, early observations using written or taped field notes can be collated to broaden the baseline criteria; areas of potential difficulty can be identified and a range of ways of supporting children's needs can be prioritized. Tracking 'significant achievement' regularly is enabled through both documents like the Foundation Stage Guidance and, broader, through StEPs as we shall see.

Using this Pack provides an additional way of observing and analysing how children can be supported and challenged by practitioners. Consider the following:

The nursery nurse, Jill, is observing a group of 4 Year R children playing in the water tray, filling and emptying a selection of containers. Rebecca pours water from a tall plastic bottle into a small boat, which quickly sinks. She looks rather anxiously at Jill but then David copies her actions using a large bottle and a medium-sized boat. When his boat too sinks, he turns to Rebecca and says: 'My boat's sunk!' 'How did you do that?' asks Jill. David and Rebecca repeat their earlier actions. Then David lifts the boat from the bottom of the tray and says, 'Look it's floating now! It's not full any more!' Jill asks, 'So what word would you use to describe that?' Rebecca joins in shouting excitedly, 'Empty – it's empty now!' Jill and the children then discuss the shape and size of the containers they've been using. When the water play ends, the children dry and paint their boats and add a written label explaining their findings.

With most Baseline Assessment Schemes, this brief observation would allow the practitioner to allocate a level based upon the current Baseline Scheme in operation by commenting upon children's:

- PSE – social interactions, ability to interact with peers and adults and take turns.
- Maths – language of full/empty, size and shape of containers.
- Language – writing individual words (e.g. boat) and mark-making.

In terms of the StEPs Pack, Entitlement 1 (described in more detail below) enables a related assessment but extends this to inform future development and practice. For example, in:

Columns A/B: SOCIAL – Child's prior knowledge...
Rebecca often appears to be a shy, sometimes insecure child, reluctant to offer her own ideas except during individual activities with an adult. She rarely contributes verbally during tasks involving small groups of peers, although she appears to observe the behaviour of others closely.

Column C: Child needs to learn about...
Working as part of a group, how to engage in relationships with peers, to build trust and security in relationships, self-respect.

Column D: Practitioner will need to know...
How to provide children with a positive self-image, about children's social development, how to create a challenging (but supportive) framework, how to identify specific individual needs.

Column E: Practitioner will make provision for...
Children to learn within different (small) groupings and individually, children to learn in a range of different contexts (e.g. water play if the child shows competence in this area).

Column F: Practitioners should teach...
Skills appropriate to Rebecca's needs, e.g. building on her competent use of vocabulary, different purposes for varied resources, respect for self and others, group skills and turn-taking.

The strength of the StEPs Pack is that there are also many aspects of other Entitlements (e.g. Entitlement 6) that equally could relate to the water play cameo (see Super Cameos in Section 7).

All assessment of this type can be undertaken in the context of *any* curriculum subject area in which the learning and teaching involve children in a social context. What is important is that the teaching is playful and child-oriented. In this spontaneous system where Rebecca was so excited about knowing the necessary vocabulary, praise from the teacher could be followed up with simple 'plays on words', making up 'nonsense' words that rhyme with empty, or the difference between this sound and Humpty, thus linking literacy teaching with a play activity.

By linking to the Social and Language Charts in the Child Development information (Section 9), it will quickly become apparent how useful these are in thinking about the targets that might be set for Rebecca following such baseline observation data.

We now move on to explore how each Entitlement covers different aspects of children's learning and development and practitioners' learning and development of professional skills and knowledge. Each Entitlement is set in the context of action within a setting and explains:

- Why the Entitlement is significant.
- How it emerged from the project.
- How it can be used to enhance and develop learning.

ENTITLEMENT 1

Young children are entitled to play experiences that engage them affectively and socially in their own and others' learning

Entitlement 1 in action

Chloë (aged 4 years) has been distressed and disturbed since the birth of her baby sister 6 weeks ago. Nursery practitioners have discussed with Chloë's mother how they might support the child in coming to terms with her new sibling. It is apparent from these discussions that the separation of Chloë from her mother has been at least part of the cause of the child's trauma. The practitioners plan the setting up of a maternity hospital in the socio-dramatic play area and invite a small group of children including Chloë to 'research' what the 'hospital' might need to care for mothers and their babies. Being part of the process of setting up and playing in the area quickly enables Chloë to express and come to terms with her feelings.

Why is E1 significant?

The dispositions and emotions of the individual must be valued and developed in the learning environment by practitioners and peers. These are an essential part of every child and will affect not only their sense of self and level of self-esteem, but also their ability to learn, in this case in the nursery setting. Practitioners need to enable what is 'inside' the individual to be transferred into a social context 'outside' of that individual, a social context within which they then have a full role. Children will be required to function throughout their lives as individuals and as part of various groups and they should learn this from an early age (Siraj-Blatchford and Clarke 2000). Play provides a major context in which children can try out their social skills, observe others' behaviours and generally understand their own and others' roles in this wider society.

How did E1 emerge from the project?

The social and affective domains of children's learning and development are areas acknowledged, accepted and emphasized by early years practitioners (Roberts 1995). Parents and practitioners are rightly concerned that children develop appropriate social skills, confidence in themselves and trust in others, realizing that, without these skills, their children are unlikely to be happy and effective learners.

The practitioner-researcher group established early in the project the importance for them of children's social development and the need for a broad range of opportunities for young children to experience different social contexts through play for their healthy mental and physical development (Bilton 1998). Whenever practitioners were challenged to justify learning through play in their settings, the development of social skills and responding to individual emotional needs were frequently cited as reasons behind their planning. While we all recognized the need for planning to take account of children's collective needs, there were many occasions in which the social needs of the individual prompted a particular type of play experience from which other children benefited by this individualized provision. In fact, the maternity hospital (in the cameo above) provided a wealth of experiences for most of the children in the nursery, including those who had new siblings 'on the way' as well as those children who don't normally encounter babies in their everyday lives.

Related to other aspects of child development, Entitlement 1 accentuates the developing knowledge, understanding and challenge children must develop of their own and others' views, ideas and responsibilities. Emotionally, children must become aware of the control they are able to command over their own and other people's feelings and responses and develop a robust approach to challenges. Children should encounter the use of language (rather than physicality) to express emotions and ideas and to relate to peers and adults (Whitehead 1999).

How can Entitlement 1 be used to enhance and develop learning?

With a sense of self as social being, children can accomplish a great deal. Emotionally it is important that children can cope with success and failure, maintaining confidence in their own ideas and strategies for learning (Merry 1998). The contents of Entitlement 1 should be part of the planning and implementation of the curriculum on a daily basis. Practitioners must acquaint themselves with how all curriculum activities and experiences will affect and involve individual children and the workings of a group; for example, how the amount or arrangement of resources will impact upon the social functioning and equilibrium of any particular group of children and the effects of this upon every child's learning opportunities (see, for example, Pascal and Bertram 1999). By thinking carefully about the social implications of a situation, the practitioner can ensure that the most efficient use of that precious commodity, time, can be made to maximize teaching and learning experiences, both for the adult and for the children. Two children can share a glue pot, but eight children sharing one glue pot is courting trouble! The practitioner-researcher group became very involved in discussions such as these and, through extensive observation and analysis of videos of our practices – for example, one instance of a group of children modelling with recycled materials – we became conscious about the influence of resources upon the social dynamics of the situation.

This Entitlement encompasses the discipline, rules and boundaries of the context for learning: it underlines the importance of self-control and self-discipline and of group identities and 'conformity' in the sense of working within the established frameworks of the social group. It is a key part of the general 'climate' of any setting and supports an ethos in which practitioners are attempting to advance clear ideas on how adults and children should show respect and regard for each other in adult/adult, adult/child and child/child contexts.

ENTITLEMENT 2

Young children are entitled to play experiences that are set in meaningful and relevant activities and contexts for learning

Entitlement 2 in action

Mike, a Year 2 teacher, involves a group of six children one lunchtime in finding references and prices for an equipment order he has to make. The children are very enthusiastic and make some excellent suggestions for useful resources. Long after the order has been placed, the children continue to look through the educational catalogues making 'ideal' order lists for themselves and quickly other children become interested. Mike decides to provide an on-going group 'ordering' activity and provides the children with telephones, catalogues, order forms and note pads, which encourages a wealth of language and mathematical development. They also use the internet to look at home shopping sites.

Why is Entitlement 2 significant?

Focusing on how and what we provide for children's learning, Entitlement 2 takes as its starting point the child's own experiences and ability to work from his or her own knowledge and skills. By using evidence about children's cultural, social, religious and ethnic background, practitioners can plan to provide activities and situations that are appropriate and allow the child to build on what they already know, can do and have experienced (Suschitzky and Chapman 1998). Instead of putting the child in the position of a 'novice' who has to start again from a low level, the child becomes an 'expert', already competent in many facets of learning. A little knowledge within the child should be an invitation to the practitioner to become involved in the child's world of learning (Fisher 1996).

A positive stance from the teacher, as in the opening cameo, initiates an equally positive stance in the learners. The child treated as a 'reader' – as soon as he or she has manipulated a book, for instance – will be encouraged in a desire to model and develop the ability to read (Whitehead 1999). The same applies to a child using pen and paper who is considered, and valued, as a writer. It also became clear to the practitioner-researcher group that a child recognizes the difference between being valued and being patronized and will respond positively or negatively to the experience accordingly.

For activities to be meaningful to children, they need to be suitable and applicable to their current ability and stage of development (Bredekamp 1987) and practitioners can identify children's individual learning needs on the basis of collective knowledge. This process is reflected in settings in many ways:

Karen and Alison, the playgroup leaders, have provided a new range of resources for the children to use in the water to link with a theme of 'babies' that they have planned as a stimulus to the children's interest in promoting care for others. They have provided dolls, towels, sponges and baby products and laid them out carefully for the children to use alongside a large water tray.

At the end of the session, Karen and Alison are surprised and concerned by the inappropriate play the children have demonstrated. For example, they were found 'drowning' the babies, putting towels in the water and using the shampoo bottles to squirt water, usually at each other!

The following day a parent visits to show the children her new baby and how to bathe it (this had been pre-planned as part of the playgroup's activities). The children watched transfixed, showing concern when the baby cried and fascination at the effects of talcum powder on wet and dry skin and the game played with the baby by the parent in 'hiding' behind the towel. From this point on, the water play modelled closely what the children had seen. They played realistically, showing the care and concern one would expect for their 'babies'.

'Babies' became *meaningful and relevant* to the children only after they had observed directly how the mother responded to her baby at bath time. This cameo demonstrates the power and importance of presenting children with activities that make 'human sense' (Donaldson 1992), especially if we expect sensitive, human responses. The initial experience allowed the practitioner to judge the children's understanding and to provide a relevant learning scenario lasting several weeks, which allowed the children to develop a wide range of subject-based knowledge and other skills.

How did Entitlement 2 emerge from the project?

This Entitlement emerged from discussion of the statement 'Learning takes place only in meaningful and relevant contexts' (Moyles 1989: 85; Wood and Attfield 1996: 70). From observing each other's practice and discussing the purposes behind our provision, it was decided that differences in these two elements are essential to reflect the child's local environment and circumstances. For example, the group held extensive discussion following a visit to one setting where a 'jungle' play area had been provided for the 4- and 5-year-olds. The main question raised was, 'How meaningful and relevant is this provision to these children?' Given that most of the children had never set foot out of a medium-sized English city, the answer had to be 'Not a lot!'

We argued that the jungle was 'broadening experiences' and 'developing imagination', but it quickly became apparent that one can only 'broaden' something on the basis of what is currently known: imagination operates from using images already in the head and extending them beyond normal boundaries (Duffy 1998). In either case, without the visual imagery gained by prior experience, the jungle could in no way be either meaningful or relevant to these particular children. A visit to a local wood accompanied by the setting up of a 'forest' area would have been a very different – and more meaningful – context. The problem is that what is meaningful and relevant to adults can sometimes be well outside children's prior experiences.

The child's life experiences and learning out of school are important features, which must act as the 'baseline' for provision in the setting or classroom. Through talking with parents and carers and using any records passed on from previous settings, plus observation of the child in the early days of entering the new context, practitioners will be able to plan a learning environment that provides starting points in experiences that offer meaning and enhance children's abilities and aptitudes as well as their on-going desire to learn.

How can Entitlement 2 be used to enhance and develop learning?

From the jungle scenario, we established that a meaningful play experience has an underpinning security for children that they have knowledge and skills, which the adults are prepared to recognize and develop. Children these days 'know' of so many things (through media of all kinds), but their knowledge is often very fragmented and can be based on a lack of real comprehension or on real investigation. There are many play contexts that have meaning for children: role play, exploratory and investigative, creative and outdoor opportunities are part of most children's natural and playful world.

We feel that practitioners should use this Entitlement as an underlying principle in their approach to developing a learning environment – if something does not make sense to this particular group of children, don't provide it! Practitioners should examine the contents of the Foundation Stage Guidance and KS1 to plan ways in which the requirements can be fulfilled keeping meaning and relevance for particular 3- to 7-year-olds in mind.

As children gain in knowledge, skills and experience, what is meaningful and relevant to them will be expanded. This means that making activities meaningful and relevant to children in itself provides a structure for enhancing children's learning. Real-life experiences, like visiting a shop, café or post office, should be provided but will need to be revisited to reinforce and enhance what children can learn from these situations. The provision of a play shop, café or post-office to extend the real-life situation will bring meaningfulness and relevance into sharp relief for young learners. The children's own active involvement in setting the provision in place can differentiate their stage of learning; this can be seen in several sections of the video.

ENTITLEMENT 3

Young children are entitled to play experiences that promote curiosity and the use of imagination and creativity in learning

Entitlement 3 in action

A group of four 3-year-olds are now familiar with playing with dry sand. A playgroup practitioner decides to join the group to try to extend and develop the play and children's language development. She begins to add water to the dry sand while the children are still involved in digging and scraping. As she pours water into one corner, the children become curious. She asks them to think of what the sand looks like on the beach when the water (tide) comes in. She encourages the children to experience, explore and express ideas, make responses and ask questions about the changing properties of the material and thus enhances their understanding of sand and the appropriate language labels to attach.

Why is Entitlement 3 significant?

Practitioners recognize that children need to be empowered to make choices, to find out, to be motivated, to investigate and to ask questions. For the next generation of 'problem-solvers' to emerge (be they artists or scientists), children from a very early age need to be encouraged to believe in themselves and their own creative potential. Trite though this can sometimes sound, practitioners must recognize that drawing outlines for children and making marks for them disempowers the artist and investigator in them (Beetlestone 1998).

When children are engaged in quality learning experiences, they are actively involved in exploring and forming a relationship that is tangible and personal with a material or a situation (de Boo 1999). This enables children to build upon previous knowledge and develops their understanding that this assimilated knowledge can be used when meeting the next challenge. Without this, challenge becomes a threat and problems become a frustration.

How did Entitlement 3 emerge from the project?

This Entitlement, covering as it does the promotion of curiosity, creativity and imagination, has been written by the practitioner-researchers and reflects the challenges faced when deconstructing and reconstructing their beliefs about the importance of play and learning. Children who have confidence in their own physical prowess will be able to manipulate and explore materials without frustration (Maude 2001). In both cases, this will promote and extend even greater capability. We discussed how an understanding of Entitlement 3 affords any practitioner a starting point to reflect on their existing practice and to expand it. It offers flexibility and universal accessibility irrespective of the setting or children because it is non-prescriptive. Practitioners can be creative and imaginative, too!

How can Entitlement 3 be used to enhance and develop learning?

The tacit structure within the Entitlement 3 Chart can enable practitioners to reflect, recognize and evaluate their own expertise as well as that of individual children. Practitioners will appreciate that there does not need to be a tangible end-product from providing good-quality teaching and learning: the process and experience of being curious and using imagination in itself challenges and takes children forward (Duffy 1998).

There is always the danger that, on the one hand, we want future citizens who can think for themselves and be curious about what happens in society and, on the other, wanting children who will do as they are told and not question too much! We would argue that, if children are encouraged early on to rationalize from the basis of their own creative thinking, it is not only in their best future interests, but provides the immediate context for reasoning with children and enabling them to make reflective and proactive decisions about their own lives. An example of this would be:

Joseph (nearly 5 years of age) digs a small hole in the sand with one finger. He says to the adult, 'This is my pond . . . the frog is at the bottom . . . he's hiding in the mud'.

Teacher: *'Do you remember visiting the pond?'*
Joseph: *'Yes, we saw . . . There were frogs jumping . . . and their legs . . . (he indicates stretching with arm movements) hopped along. I want water . . . here . . . this is my pond'.*

He goes to fetch water and brings back half a cupful in a bucket, pours it into his pond. It fills the space exactly, but he watches as the water is soaked up by the sand. He goes again, fetches the same amount, pours and watches as the same thing happens again. He looks at the teacher and pauses.

Teacher: *'What would you like to do now?'*
Joseph: *'Get some more'.*

He fetches half a bucketful and pours it into his 'pond'. It overflows and he watches the water as it soaks into the surrounding sand.

Joseph: *'I can't make a pond here . . . the sand . . . it's sucking it up . . . all of my water'.*
Teacher: *'Can you stop the sand sucking up your water?*
Joseph: *'I could . . . could get all the stones and shells . . . and put them round my pond . . . the water would . . . would . . . ?*
Teacher: *'What do you think would happen to the water . . . try it . . . and see?'*

ENTITLEMENT 4

Young children are entitled to engage in play experiences that are open-ended and offer trial-and-error learning without fear of failure

Entitlement 4 in action

Four children are using a programmable toy (Roamer) to recreate the story of 'Don't Forget the Bacon' (Shirley Hughes). Two of them are Year 1 children and they each have a Year 4 'partner'. These two children gather relevant resources from a display of pretend eggs, cakes, peas, bacon and other 'goodies' supplied by the practitioner, which they place along a pathway. The Year 1 children take delight in trying to decide how to collect all of the relevant articles in the correct sequence by programming the Roamer under the guidance of their partners. After a few 'false starts' and much laughter and discussion among the partners, the items are eventually gathered according to the story.

Why is Entitlement 4 significant?

It is now well accepted that young children need not only be given opportunities to play at their own level of development, but that this level can be enhanced by practitioners prepared to 'scaffold' their learning in the context of Vygotsky's 'zone of proximal development' (Kozulin 1998). Other more knowledgeable children can also act as 'scaffolders' as in the cameo above. There is also a general recognition that we all learn most effectively through trial and error, meaning that we can try out from the basis of what we already know and make mistakes in order to understand what we still need to learn and to do. Play offers a non-threatening context in which to learn to 'cope with new learning and still retain self-esteem and self-image' (Moyles 1994: 7; Lindon 1993).

Practitioners who promote an enquiry-based classroom ethos entitle children to experience success and failure in a safe, secure environment and support children's experimentation within familiar and unfamiliar contexts. Having such opportunities ensures that children explore their own constructs and theories of the world and challenge themselves to master techniques and ideas without constraints of time. We need children like those described by Fisher (1996: 7): 'Young children [who] display motivation and determination . . . they want to succeed . . . they demonstrate persistence and perseverance. The desire to find out and do is so strong that children will try over and over again – through failure after failure – to succeed'.

Therein, you may say, lies the problem! We have already noted previously that any prescribed curriculum can dominate time and content in ways that may not always be helpful to children's learning. This pressure on time often happens for practitioners and children because we all insist on trying to fit new initiatives on top of old ones rather than reconsidering practice (Galton et al. 1999). StEPs in itself – once users are familiar – can be thought of as capable of supporting other planning and developmental systems operating in settings to implement the statutory and recommended curricula.

How did Entitlement 4 emerge from the project?

Children cannot be hurried: this was one of our clear messages to each other during the period of the research. From whichever angle we viewed the situation, it became clear, especially from video analysis, observation and discussion, that if children are to succeed they must be given space and time to come to their own decisions. Without the time to become involved for long periods with their own investigations, children appear to learn in only shallow and inconsistent ways, whereas given time to develop their ideas and skills, it is remarkable how competent even the youngest children can become.

The responsible adult will recognize when more time is needed and find ways around the constraints of time. Usually this happens by recognizing what different aspects of the curriculum are being covered at any one time by a 'single' activity, as in the following example.

Liz, a Year R teacher, has recently realized the children's interest in the local building site which most of them pass every day on their way to school. She decides to capitalize on this interest by suggesting that the children bring a 'person' (some kind of toy figure) from home to take part in a construction activity at school. The following morning Liz makes available a selection of construction materials and suggests to the children that they should construct a building in which the toy figure might 'live'. Liz herself brings in a small teddy bear and builds a home for it, modelling for the children her own thinking and asking for their ideas to improve teddy's house. Children quickly use this strategy for themselves, discussing animatedly the size of their figures and the appropriateness of different constructional materials.

Originally, 45 minutes had been allowed for this construction session but, as Liz observed the level of perseverance and motivation, she decided to extend the activity into a session on the following day. A reflective session at the end with the children convinced her that this was appropriate use of time, particularly as many of the children had ideas to both extend and develop their constructions further and others wanted the chance to try something different.

The following morning, about a third of the children brought different toys and made other various 'houses' while the rest of the children continued the process from the previous day, absorbed in developing suitable buildings, and hunting for further materials to enhance their constructions.

Saving constructions for the following day's sessions by using an area that did not have to be cleared at the end of the day, enabled children to begin to understand time and provided an example of realistic time scales in which activities could be pursued to a satisfactory conclusion.

How can Entitlement 4 be used to enhance and develop learning?

As can be seen, the building activity covers many different aspects of learning and development:

Social: children concentrate, persevere, make choices, recognize their own and others' needs.
Physical: fine motor coordination, extending physical capabilities.
Emotional: self-motivation, perseverance, confidence in experimentation, security within success and failure when solving problems, valuing own and others' ideas.
Intellectual: spatial awareness, consolidating and extending knowledge of structures, evaluating and

re-evaluating own actions and outcomes, estimating size, restructuring ideas and raising and solving problems, seeking help from adults and peers.

Linguistic: communicating with confidence and expression, verbalizing own experiences, listening to others, questioning, articulating ideas.

The building cameo also shows children engaged within several aspects of the Foundation Stage Guidance, such as knowledge and understanding of the world (design and technology focus, knowledge of materials and fitness for purpose), creative and physical, with some numeracy and literacy components.

ENTITLEMENT 5

Young children are entitled to playful, exploratory and experiential activities with a variety of materials and resources and within a variety of contexts

Entitlement 5 in action

The scene is a socio-dramatic play area set up as a baker's shop. A group of 4½ year-olds have visited a local bakery to buy currant buns, which they have promptly eaten! Back in their own shop, they realize that they do not have any currant buns for sale. They discuss with the practitioner what they can do and decide jointly that making some 'play buns' would be helpful in stocking their shop. The practitioner makes available the materials for the production of dough and the children proceed with the making of the buns, discussing what they should put in them to represent currants, what colours and textures they need to be, the cost of the ingredients, the sale price, and so on.

Why is Entitlement 5 significant?

Of all the Entitlements, this is the one that will perhaps be most readily acknowledged by practitioners. Cognitive psychologists have now been offering evidence for many decades that all learners need to experience exploration of materials and ideas as a preliminary 'data gathering' exercise (Claxton 1998). With basic knowledge and skills acquired through exploration, it is then possible to gain further understanding through applying current knowledge. As Edwards and Knight (1994: 73) point out, 'There is a lot of redundancy in learning. By this we mean that it may take several attempts before we grasp something and that it will then take a lot of practice before we become confident or skilled with it'. In the baker's shop play, the children's opportunity to extend their initial experience through having the shop area in their classroom and their experience in both having the real currant buns and making others for their own play use, allowed the children to interact and engage with the learning environment in a playful and enjoyable way.

Entitlement 5 reflects one of the main ways in which learning in young children occurs – by hands-on, practical, play experiences. It matches appropriately their stage of development and preferred learning method. As one of our group put it, 'Play is where children are, so why don't we capitalize on it rather than fighting it?' Children's learning is based on their own interactions with their own environment, planned, supported and guided by knowledgeable adults (Anning and Edwards 1999). By handling, observing, investigating and questioning through one's own first-hand discoveries, children practise and test their knowledge, understanding and skills. They also test their aptitude and attitude towards learning, appraising their skills against peers.

How did Entitlement 5 emerge from the project?

There was general recognition within the group that settings need to provide a variety of contexts where children can be adventurous. The situation in society as a whole at present is a cause for concern, as pointed out in a Barnardo's Report (1995): children are increasingly restricted in their opportunities to take risks and learn from their own endeavours for a variety of reasons. With increasing levels of traffic, children are often confined to their own homes and gardens. More readily available and affordable computers and the extended use of video and television mean that even the youngest children often spend several hours a day in front of screens, which can be detrimental physically, emotionally, socially and intellectually and mean that vital personal communication skills may not be developed effectively (see Healy 1998; Cook and Finlayson 1999). While we all believe firmly in computers and the internet as a means of communication in itself, young children will only realize the potential of such systems when they understand all forms of communication from a first-hand, experiential basis – this seems like yet another process we are trying to 'hurry' in children (Elkind 1988).

The research group also found that they were very 'hooked' into resource provision for children without a clear understanding of what such resources provided for children's learning. There was a comparatively vague notion, for example, of why *do* we provide home areas? And this was not the only question! Even when we had decided that they are provided, among other things, to:

- support the transition between home and school;
- enable children to have a meaningful but imaginative context in which to play;
- offer opportunities for social language;
- enable children to take on a variety of everyday roles;
- encourage children to respond to different social contexts by the variety of resources supplied;
- enable the adult to challenge stereotypical roles by provision and interaction;

we were still left with other questions, such as: Do my home area resources reflect the home backgrounds of all the children? Do the materials reflect different cultures and traditions? Am I able to provide resources that reflect a full range of curricular intentions? What do I do to encourage social development in the home area? Do I ever take on a role in the home area to extend children's activities beyond the mundane and routine?

For one of the practitioner-researchers, Jill, a main concern during the project has been with appropriate and effective provision for learning within the socio-dramatic play area of the classroom. As she explained:

> In the past a home area in the classroom has materialized, as far as the children are concerned, overnight. Consequently, how I envisaged the children would interact with the resources didn't happen because within two minutes all the hard work I'd put in was in a pile on the floor! On reflection, I decided on a different approach. Not only did it have to be meaningful and relevant, but I had also got to let the children explore and experiment with the materials so as to give them a sense of ownership over the area – to make it their own.

Many readers will empathize with this dilemma. While it takes time for children to be involved in developing this type of area, it is time well spent because of the ways in which children not only extend their thinking by planning and making some of their own provision for play, but because they gain an important sense that their views and ideas are respected and valued by practitioners.

Jill went on to explain what happened when she engaged the children in development of a supermarket play area:

> Having discussed with the children what happened in supermarkets, they were able to express lots of ideas of what they needed as they had familiar language in which to describe familiar supermarkets and shops. They were able to select the resources needed and they could determine the roles that should be adopted by individuals. This discussion also gave me the opportunity to offer input and to challenge the children before they became totally involved in the play in ways which extended what then happened. I was also able to use this opportunity to assess what children already knew and was then in a better position to extend the play by making suggestions to specific children.
>
> By taking this experiential approach to play area provision, I found the children's play was much more consistent; it flowed a lot easier and it allowed me access in a player role when I became the delivery person or the shelf stacker (doing it for pin money, of course!) or the shop manager, rather than having to direct the play or get the children to take on roles of my choosing.

Even as adults, we have to allow ourselves the time to experiment with and explore new things. Learning to use a new piece of equipment is enabled so much better if there is someone to help set it up, if questions are posed and decision-making undertaken and if you, yourself, are engaged directly.

Working through the contents of the Entitlement 5 Chart you will be nurturing children's use of senses in investigating the world and developing their intellectual and linguistic skills, such as questioning, discriminating, decision-making and formulating ideas. A hands-on approach also ensures that children make emotional responses to their actions and reactions, which, in turn, as Goleman (1996) has shown, stimulates particular aspects of brain development.

How can Entitlement 5 be used to enhance and develop learning?

Entitlement 5 permits children to be central in their own learning. Adults will at times act as a role model, thus enabling children to review and reflect on their activities through seeing someone else engaged in the investigative process. Practitioners can show fun and enjoyment in what they are doing, thus justifying learning as a spontaneous and joyful on-going event.

In thinking through provision using Entitlement 5, several of the group made some interesting discoveries.

> In my setting we found that we had to think much more carefully about the type and amount of resources we provided for the children. Sometimes this meant adding materials to areas so that – thinking about the social development aspect of this Entitlement – more children could become involved in exploration and investigation as a joint enterprise.

> Equality of experience in my setting meant that we had to ensure that not only did all children have access to exploratory and investigative play, but that this was 'matched' to their current developmental level. One child with very good mathematical skills, for example, spontaneously explored different ways of making 100 with a pack of lollipop sticks that were really intended for the creative area.

> We rotate our involvement in the exploratory and investigative activities because we have found that different children respond differently to individual adults, with some children being far more experimental in the presence of some practitioners than others. By rotating, we ensure that most children get a range of experiences from any one activity.

> During observation sessions, we have noticed that, by offering a variety of construction equipment, it allows the children to experience the area of play but at many different levels and with a variety of responses. For example, we found that small, linking construction bricks tended to be played with individually, whereas the large unit blocks seem to invite children to be more experimental in groups.

Clearly, these comments indicate that provision of resources and materials for hands-on experiences should be limited without being limiting because what is provided can affect the type of exploratory play to which the children are entitled. Being able to internalize and visualize through earlier hands-on activities acts as the bedrock for the move into symbolism, which is so vital if children are to become literate and numerate. It is well known that ample opportunities for this type of learning reap substantial benefits in the long term in learners who can think and act quickly and intelligently (Claxton 1998).

ENTITLEMENT 6

Young children are entitled to engage in individual and dynamic play and learning experiences relevant to their age group and stage of development

Entitlement 6 in action

> *Two children – a 4+ child (Stephen) and a Year 6 child (Louise) – are together exploring a selection of magnets and magnetic/non-magnetic items in an area of the classroom. Stephen is absorbed in his exploration of the materials, repeating and providing a running commentary on his actions. Each time Louise tries to intervene, he rejects her offers but continues to watch as she succeeds in linking a string of paper clips by gently stroking them on a magnet. When he has succeeded in collecting a long string of paper clips for himself, Stephen turns to Louise, who is kneeling next to him, and pulls at her sleeve to show her how he has made a 'snake'. He proceeds to pull the snake towards Louise, saying 'Look, look . . . it's coming to get you . . . Ssssss!'*

Why is Entitlement 6 significant?

Children benefit from opportunities to learn and play individually and through intellectual interaction with objects, materials, other people and with groups of peers across gender, cultures and abilities. Empowerment to learn means being given opportunities to learn in a mentally and physically stimulating and exciting way.

Socially, children need an in-depth knowledge of themselves: how they will respond to different situations, whether they will throw a temper tantrum or be able to cope with, for example, separation, will determine what they will be able to experience from the various play and learning opportunities available to them in the setting. This implies a sound knowledge of their own strategies for learning and for coping – metacognitive awareness, as it is now called in a wide range of literature (see, for example, Wood 1998).

Children's inherent appreciation of the joy and satisfaction of learning and achieving is a prerequisite for working within Entitlement 6: developing control of one's own emotions and reactions will serve as a necessary foundation for all learning skills and strategies.

How did Entitlement 6 emerge from the project?

Of all the Entitlements, this one has caused most problems for us as practitioners. We have tried continually to find another word to replace 'dynamic' but there appears to be nothing which supplants this word with its connotations of continual change, drive, energy, vibrance, invigoration, interaction and liveliness – all rolled into this one word.

This Entitlement is derived from one of the original 'principles of play' developed by the practitioner-researchers, namely that play is 'an expression of individual choice and freedom'. Play is owned or decided upon individually or collectively by children. That it is motivated by choice and children can become involved in it or not means that play offers excitement within a personal framework for children. This does not mean (as we shall see) that adults have no role to play – far from it!

Children are entitled to be *enthralled* by play that is lively, vital, go-getting, active and powerful for them. They are entitled, too, to respond at a personal level to experiences that are pertinent, distinctive and essentially idiosyncratic. They are entitled to become personally motivated as instigators of their own individualized learning, be it with or without associated players. By observation it is possible to monitor individual and group use of resources and withhold judgement on the validity of the play scenario. Cross-referencing observations with the child development documents enables practitioners to evaluate and plan using the children's competence and provide for extension in developing learning further (Hutchin 1996).

How can Entitlement 6 be used to enhance and develop learning?

We acknowledge that children compare, evaluate, predict, rehearse and consolidate knowledge and skills with the support of others as well as personally. The adult's understanding of how the child has evolved his or her social skills to any given point and, as crucially, what they can anticipate as future achievement for this individual, is the basis upon which planning for Entitlement 6 will take place. If we expect dynamic interactions, then we need to understand what is likely to prompt them.

The other issue is that of 'rules' and how often children set 'rules' without fully understanding the underlying concept of 'fairness'. Rules are socially inspired but are easily broken by younger children, which can cause tensions in relationships. Children's constructs are shaped by what they have previously encountered in family and community and this will be unique to each child. Ensuring that these different experiences can become socially and dynamically linked within a setting is a significant role for practitioners.

The dynamic nature of play needs careful planning by adults as it is easy for activities to become mundane, individualized and 'dull' for children. An example would be the increasing use of page after page of 'worksheet'-based exercises, which neither challenge nor inspire children's learning and could be said to be positively harmful in the sense of disallowing both interaction with others and the kind of innovation and enervation that makes play just what it is.

In play contexts, it is easy to see children's sense of self-worth – the 'can-do' child in a 'can-do' curriculum (Moyles 2001). Children who are reluctant to play are often those who feel that they have more to lose, emotionally, by trying rather than by being merely a spectator. Yet to be fully active in the learning process, children need to overcome these fears of failure and engage both individually and within groups as in the following cameo:

> A mixed-ability group of Year 2 children – two boys and two girls – are using salt dough they made on the previous day to make items for the class café. For the first 2–3 minutes, they explore the dough's possibilities, stretching and pulling it. But then Rashid quickly decides that what is needed is some naan bread. He has to explain to the rest of the group about naan bread and that it has a particular (teardrop) shape. This appears not to be understood by the others in the group and Rashid looks both frustrated and disappointed with his fellow players. They argue for a few minutes over what the shape looks like – they can see nothing like it around the room. The adult notices and brings over to them paper and pencil, suggesting to Rashid that he might draw the shape so the other children will understand. Rashid reluctantly decides that it's easier to demonstrate. Using his outline as a template he rolls his dough on to the paper, watched closely by the others, and then proceeds rather precariously to cut around both the dough and the paper. Sarah, upon seeing this, suggests that an easier way is to cut out the paper first. All four children agree and cut their own shapes from paper, using these to shape their pieces of dough. They call the teacher to check how their naan bread can be baked ready for use in the café. 'What is naan bread?', she asks. The other children all look to Rashid, who carefully (and proudly) explains how his family make and eat naan bread.

As practitioners we observe and assess the children and are acutely aware of the range of social developmental levels within which the children operate. Through observation we can highlight and increase opportunities for peer group recognition that the more reluctant and less confident child might need assistance or reassurance. Rules are determined by people and the environment and developing these sensitively with the children will allow them still to retain autonomy and ownership of the play so that it retains its dynamism and relativity.

FINALE

These, then, are the six Entitlements to Play. It should be emphasized that they are also an entitlement to teach playfully and enjoyably, for practitioners have an equal right to work and play with young children without fear of reproach for such practices. This situation carries the need, however, for practitioners to be able to articulate clearly **why** their practice is play-based and what benefits this accrues for the children as the foundation for current and future learning. The following section extends the rationale behind the entitlements through identifying what constitutes good practice within the StEPs.

SECTION SEVEN

Using the six entitlements: interpreting StEPs in action in the setting

The aims of this section are to:
- Detail the practicalities of how StEPs actually operates in effective, everyday early years practices.
- Exemplify the learning content and quality of experiences of both children and practitioners through sensitive interpretation of the StEPs framework.
- Show how the Entitlements can be linked through a broad range of teaching and learning experiences.

To explain and elaborate anything, there is nothing like a good story. We have chosen to elucidate the six Entitlements through 'stories', which we have called 'cameos of excellence'. Like the practice shown on the video, they represent both good practice and high standards of learning and teaching in early years settings. They are not 'models' of how to do, but examples of quality play and learning for children and exciting and innovative playful teaching by practitioners.

We have used cameos from a range of contexts to include children up to 7 years of age. The practitioner-researcher group feel strongly that KS1 is in danger of being 'forgotten' as a developmental phase in children's lives in the downward pressure to conform to KS2 requirements. It is our opinion that this should be resisted vigorously by teachers and support staff in KS1 classes because of everything we know about the developing child and the consistency of practice and provision that is necessary for all young children. Throughout primary school, children require wide-ranging practical, hands-on experiences similar to those provided for younger children but with additional challenge and increasing peer collaboration. The growing brain is still craving for the kind of stimulation provided within play-based learning experiences both to extend and to deepen the neurological pathways and connections that have been growing apace in the earlier years (Kotulak 1996; POST 2000). As importantly, the child's growing body is thirsting to expend energy in physical ways; time spent passively sitting filling in worksheets can amount to cruelty to children in KS1 who, above all else, are exuberant about life in general and are keen to throw themselves wholeheartedly, mentally and physically into learning activities. Practitioners must capitalize on this energy and ensure that teaching and learning match the challenge.

Several cameos are presented under each Entitlement to Play Statement. Each StEP starts with the **context** being outlined, followed by the **story** itself. This is then elaborated to show:

- what the children are likely to be learning;
- what the practitioner's role is;
- what progression and continuity might be considered (where to now?);
- what links with child development are evident;
- what links with the Foundation Stage Guidance and/or KS1 can be made.

In presenting the first and second of these, readers will find particular statements underlined. Our intention here is to show you the direct links to be made with the contents of the Entitlement Charts. In the case of the third point, the practitioner-researchers have identified how they handle progression to show the importance of considering the next steps. Child development links relate directly to our charts in Section 9. Foundation Stage Guidance and KS1 links are included to help those of you whose planning is likely to start from the basis of the contents of these documents.

While age groups of children are given in each cameo to enable readers to understand clearly the setting for these particular learners and practitioners, the activities can be conceived as being suitable for a wide range of age groups once attention is paid to children's current developmental level and background experiences. Herein lies the key to the StEPs pack – or, should we say, its ladder? Provided practitioners are working from the basis of children's prior knowledge and experience and they bring to bear their own knowledge and prior understanding of the particular children with whom they currently play and work, it is easy to match future teaching and learning opportunities to what has gone before in any of the specific contexts described in our 'stories' of good practice. Additionally, although it is possible to replicate particular activities and learning environments, it is vital that practitioners stop to ask themselves what their intentions would be behind making such provision: How will the children's learning benefit from this experience? What do practitioners need to know? What planning is needed to ensure progression and continuity? These are, of course, the very questions which, if answered carefully, are the basis of quality curricular provision.

The concluding part of this Section is what we have called 'Super Cameo' – that is, it extends the ideas in the previous cameos of using a single Entitlement as the basis of learning and teaching and illustrates the way the framework can be used flexibly across the entitlements.

A WORD ABOUT PLANNING TO LINK CURRICULUM INTENTIONS WITH StEPs

Needless to say, as early years practitioners, planning comes very high on our list of priorities.

USING THE SIX ENTITLEMENTS: INTERPRETING StEPs IN ACTION IN THE SETTING

Like many of you, we 'agonize' between overly long and complex planning (ostensibly) to meet OfSTED inspection requirements and the kind of brief but adequate planning that we need to meet children's needs on a daily basis. In working with the StEPs framework, we have found that the following is the most suitable process:

- **Long-term plans** are often most straightforward if they spring directly from Foundation Stage Guidance or KS1 of the National Curriculum.
- **Medium-term plans** 'grow' effectively from each of the six Entitlement Charts and can be readily linked to long-term plans.
- **Short-term plans** are made on the basis of a particular day's activities and follow from the idea of 'what comes next?' in relation to the development of the medium-term plans.

Other examples of medium- and short-term planning are shown in the video section (Section 4; you could replicate any of these as useful blank proformas for your own purposes). As you will see, the practitioners have identified elements from within both the Foundation Stage Guidance and the KS1 curriculum documents and subsumed these within their own identification of learning from each of the cameos. Some aspects quote directly from the documents; others are adapted to fit the particular circumstances.

ENTITLEMENT 1

Young children are entitled to play experiences that engage them affectively and socially in their own and others' learning

CAMEO E1

Context

In a Year 1 class, a group of four children have recently become interested in developing a role play theme based on a story about princes and princesses. Something in the story has captured their imagination and they can frequently be found in the library area of the classroom reading the story to each other and speaking in character voices. On this particular – and fine weather – day, they have been given the opportunity to decide what activity they would like to do during outdoor play activities and have chosen to make a 'den'. Quickly, however, as will be seen, the play returns to the issue of princesses and palaces.

Balraj, Carrie-Anne, Zaitun and Nathan are playing outside in the covered play area making a 'den' by draping saris across fixed ropes, held together with clothes' pegs.

'Come on! Come on in – we've done it!' says Balraj, who appears to be 'in charge'. She speaks further to the others: 'You've got to come in and we'll close the door'.

Zaitun: *It's not a door . . . it's shiny.*
Balraj: *Yes, it's not a house. It's a palace because it's shiny and we're princesses and we live here. Come in!*

The adult who has been observing this activity approaches, at first to listen to the conversation and note the children's language use, but quickly gets drawn in.

Zaitun: *(to the adult) That's not an ordinary door.*
Adult: *Oh! Can I come in?*
Carrie-Anne: *If you're coming, you have to come in on the other side. Look, it's shiny. It's not a house – it's a palace . . . and we're princesses.*
Adult: *Can I come into your palace, then?*
Carrie-Anne: *No, because you're not a princess. You're an old woman!*
Adult *(now adopting a role)*: *Yes, I'm really a wicked demon come to take away the princess.*
Zaitun: *Why do you want to take away the princess?*
Adult *(in an evil voice)*: *Because she's beautiful and I want to lock her away so no-one will see her beauty.*
Carrie-Anne: *She is beautiful. She's Sita in the story but she's safe in our magic palace. You can't come in.*
Adult *(in a threatening manner)*: *I'll come back and capture her when you're not looking!*

The children all burst into laughter and huddle inside their 'palace'.

What were the children learning?

The children are learning to *operate within a group*, to *reason with others* and to *negotiate and cooperate*. They are *developing sophisticated social skills in a variety of contexts*. Although led by Balraj, her inclusion of other children allows them to *explore* and *respond* to the experience. The children are learning to *build trust and security in relationships*, both with each other and with the adult. They are also developing self-respect – leaders and those invited to join in are valued. The children have been given the opportunity to *choose and use resources independently*. The children *listen* to each other and *initiate ideas*. They are *confident in the worth of their own ideas and enthusiastic* about these. They are highly successful in developing the 'den'. They show an *understanding of different perspectives* in their role play as well as exhibiting a *sense of humour*. The children learn initially to *handle different materials and tools* (large sheets of fabric, rope and pegs) in a unique way, with *increasing control and coordination*. The skills they applied enable them to extend their social play with *imagination and creativity*, and they are able to *communicate their feelings without fear of failure* both within the peer group and with the adult. They talk about their experiences and link the prior story directly with their play through the use of *appropriate language and questioning and listening* skills.

What was the practitioner's role?

The practitioner provided *specific resources* outside to encourage imaginative play (the box of drapes, mats, pegs, string and tapes) and *enabled the children to initiate* their own activity. The practitioner *extended the social play* through *posing the problem* of the princess being taken away by a demon, by taking on this role. She *allowed time* for the children to engage in trial-and-error play, she *intervened* to develop the play and became a *co-player*, accepted by the children because of the way in which she engaged immediately with their story. By being *involved in this indirect way*, she was able *sensitively to question* the children and *develop their fantasy play*, providing *security and stability* for the quieter child while, at the same time, *reinforcing and extending* the capable child in her reflection of literary analogy. The *materials stimulated cooperative play* and ensured the *children interacted with each other* and *collaborated* to own the imaginative play 'palace' they had created.

Where to now?

The story is clearly capable of further expansion, with the children encouraged to plot how to keep the princess safe. They could decide that one of them is the princess and dress her in this role, requiring thought on the appropriacy of certain *materials for this purpose*. The practitioner may prompt them to write 'Keep out – no demons allowed in here' type notices or develop their story theme through paintings or drawings. The practitioner could teach about *challenging stereotypical roles* through a discussion of who is to be the 'rescuer' (male or female?). She may want to explore with the children *ideas about gender*, looks and valuing differences. The activity could be developed with older children into a more stage-managed and scripted play. The children could plan a cast of characters, a selection of props and draft a script. This could further be developed into performing their play for an audience. The practitioner can develop this level of interest into learning about the wider world (e.g. other countries – where did the story come from?) and about other stories in the genre of fantasy, thereby developing their understanding of abstract ideas. The practitioner can develop higher level language by encouraging children to experiment with different tones, volume and accents. The practitioner can also develop the children's knowledge of language associated with a particular literary genre.

Child development links

Socially the children:

- are showing that they can cooperate individually to achieve a group goal;
- can share fantasies;
- can engage in pretend play to help overcome fears;
- are using their imaginations to transport themselves to a different time and place.

Emotionally the children:

- are making decisions and planning and enjoying this process;
- are asking 'What sort of person am I?' (leader/follower, male/female, beautiful/wicked);
- are developing opinions formed by their own feelings.

Intellectually the children:

- are interested in a specific topic;
- are using their own thinking and ideas;
- are showing a detailed knowledge of a particular genre.

Linguistically the children:

- are enjoying playing with language;
- are aware of language spoken in different ways and in a different genre.

What links can be made with the KS1 curriculum?

KS1 English states that children should learn:

- to speak clearly, fluently and confidently to different people;
- to listen and respond to others;
- to join in as members of a group.

KS1 Drama states that children should learn:

- to participate in a range of drama activities;
- to use language and actions to explore and convey situations, characters and emotions;
- to create and sustain roles individually and when working with others.

Page 44 of the National Curriculum Handbook (QCA 2000c) States that English at KS1 refers to building on Foundation Stage Guidance. The cameo and its development can create links with all areas but particularly with Speaking and Listening and Drama.

ENTITLEMENT 2

Young children are entitled to play experiences that are set in meaningful and relevant activities and contexts for learning

CAMEO E2

Context

With the help of Rose, the classroom assistant, four children in a Year 1 classroom have recently visited a local café. Together the adult and children have explored the physical environment, including the kitchen, and have ordered and paid for their own food and drink. They have sat in the café as customers for a short time, talking informally about what is happening and what they observe. Rose has responded to the children's spontaneous interests and understanding and listened to their retelling of previous experiences. Rose and Heelin, the teacher, follow-up the visit by providing a classroom café for socio-dramatic play opportunities. Together they plan the types of experiences it will be useful for children to extend and consider the language that children are likely to use and that which may need to be taught. They then work with the children to develop an appropriate area of the classroom for the purpose.

The café becomes the focus of attention for all the children, not just the four who made the previous visit. Those who were part of the earlier experience, however, are observed to be taking on clearly defined roles and to be using the language reinforced or introduced during the real café experience. Early on, these children negotiate which roles they will adopt: Sabina and Amjah take the roles of customers, making sure that they have purses and money before going to the café. Ranjeet is the owner and he organizes the tables and takes orders, using a pad and pen to both write and draw the food that is required. Hamza is in the kitchen taking the orders and making up plates of food. The play lasts for 25 minutes.

The practitioners allow the children time to discuss their opinions on the organization of the café and explain their views to others. They also give time for children to settle into their roles and dictate the direction of the play before they attempt any intervention. However, observing that the customers are not always getting appropriate attention, the classroom assistant takes on the role of a customer herself. The children immediately relate to her in this role, Ranjeet giving her the menu and taking her order, Hamza making her meal. The nursery nurse refuses to eat a sausage that has been dropped on the floor and the café 'owner' is duly apologetic. After eating her meal, the 'customer' pays her bill and leaves. The children continue their play.

There are several times during the play when children check with each other how to spell words or what is the first sound of items in a particular menu order. The teacher and classroom assistant are both drawn into this in their role as 'teacher' and, because this is the children's decision, it does not affect their engagement in, or commitment to, the play. The children together spell out c-u-p and t-e-a and, at one point, there is a long discussion on whether 'you' rhymes with 'menu'. The word 'chips' presents no spelling problems, but 'sausage' is another matter altogether!

What were the children learning?

The children are engaged in a *meaningful and relevant* context. They are *linking the real, outside world* with the school setting. Having enjoyed the visit, they have a great deal of *fun and satisfaction* in *sharing their experiences* with the rest of the group. They are able to *verbalize and convey their ideas* throughout the visit and in the classroom. Playing in the classroom café, they show *respect and trust* of others; they *compromise* and *share* the play and the characters. They engage in an extended socio-dramatic play experience, *negotiating roles, persevering and concentrating*, linking their *real-life experiences* to their play. The practitioner is readily and naturally drawn into their play and is able to extend the discussion to health issues. The children 'naturally' incorporate *literacy* activities into the play – labels, menus, orders, special offers – as well as *mathematical* activities – money, adding bills, organizing rotas and counting. In pricing the menu items, the children *negotiate* their idea of appropriate cost and request one of the adult's views on £5 as an appropriate cost for sausage and chips.

What is the practitioner's role

The KS1 practitioners have *knowledge of the children's prior experiences* and make appropriate *provision for extension and development*, thus allowing the children the opportunity to *transfer real-life skills* to their socio-dramatic play. They have *motivated* the children through the visit to the café and have developed in the children *observation and interpretation skills*. They have enabled the children to use *clearly defined roles with understanding* and to use new *vocabulary* for the purpose. In observing the children, the practitioners have learned more about the way children respond to adopting roles requiring leadership skills and those required in providing a service. In using the children themselves to create the café setting, the practitioners have promoted children's development of *design and technology* skills and allowed them a significant level of *independence and decision-making*. By engaging herself in the café play, Rose has *modelled appropriate behaviour* and increased children's understanding of *health issues*. Both Rose and Heelin have been in a position directly to teach literacy and numeracy skills in a meaningful and relevant situation which children can readily understand.

What are the child development links?

Socially the children:

- are cooperating individually to achieve a group goal;
- are using their imaginations to transport themselves out of the school setting;
- are playing at a higher level of social collaboration;
- are realizing that their play is becoming more stage-managed and scripted;
- are beginning to demand more detail and accuracy in the play props.

Physically the children:

- are demonstrating their ability to form letters correctly;
- produce print that is readable by others and drawing that can be recognized by others.

Emotionally the children:

- are cooperating, sharing an understanding of role play rules and fair play;
- are skilled in making decisions and being involved in planning;
- are modelling their behaviour on that of respected adults;
- are demonstrating growing knowledge about adult expectations of dealing with food and how we eat.

Intellectually the children:

- are concentrating for longer periods to develop their ideas;
- know that print communicates meaning;
- have an interest in a specific topic and some are showing a detailed knowledge;
- are sharing early understanding of money and giving change.

Linguistically the children:

- are using language to describe, question, guess, explain, justify and complain;
- are beginning to consider an audience when writing.

What links with KS1 can be made?

KS1 Personal/Social/Emotional and Citizenship states that children should learn:

- to share their opinions on things that matter . . . and explain their views;
- to think about themselves, learn from their experiences and recognize what they are good at;
- to agree to follow rules for their group and classroom and understand how rules help them;
- to realize that people . . . have needs and that they have responsibilities to meet them;

- to realize that money comes from different sources and can be used for different purposes;
- to maintain personal hygiene;
- to recognize how their behaviour affects other people;
- to listen... play and work cooperatively;
- take and share responsibility;
- meet and talk with people... outside visitors.

KS1 – Literacy suggests that children should learn:

- to read and use captions, e.g. labels;
- to read and following simple instructions;
- to write captions for their own work;
- to make simple lists for planning, reminding, etc.;
- to write and draw simple instructions and labels for classroom use, e.g. in role play area.

The National Curriculum Handbook (QCA 2000c: 66), 'Breadth of Study', suggests that pupils should be taught knowledge, skills and understanding through:

- practical activity, exploration and discussion;
- using mathematical ideas in practical activities, then recording these;
- activities that encourage them to make connections between number work and other aspects of their work in mathematics.

ENTITLEMENT 3

Young children are entitled to play experiences that promote curiosity and the use of imagination and creativity in learning

CAMEO E3

Context

In a full-time nursery class, the practitioner opens a parcel at the table. Inside are two large fresh fish. A large group of children are invited to inspect, touch, smell and talk about it. The children begin to touch and retract their fingers rapidly. They react verbally about what they think it feels like, expressing distaste. To target their observation and encourage them to experience a different sensation, the practitioner asks them to touch the fish and think about its texture and feel. With growing confidence they start to use magnifiers of different sizes which the practitioner makes available.

Anjum: Look. Look it's got teeth.
Emily: Where? Let me see.

Anjum moves the fish to enable Emily and the other children to view the teeth.

Anjum: Look, there inside, it's a tongue, it's a tongue.

All the children peer down and inspect the fish head in great detail.

What were the children learning?

The children began to *explore and respond to sensory experiences*, to *cope with different feelings* and to *respond to a range of immediate stimuli*. Children are using their senses to explore something that is familiar and yet new and are *making observations* about it. Children are beginning to use observation tools appropriately. The children are *developing their communication skills* when *listening to each other* and *expressing their own personal feelings* about the new experience.

What is the practitioner's role?

The practitioner provided a novel resource linked with the current theme of skeletons to *stimulate and challenge* the children. She *enabled the children to experiment* and *gain confidence* in handling the fish. She gave the children opportunities to discuss their experience and *explore safely* and sensitively. By extending the activity, the practitioner allowed the children to express and communicate their ideas, thoughts and feelings imaginatively and creatively.

Where to now?

This initial activity led to the practitioner enabling the children to explore and develop the theme in the creative area of the curriculum. The children (and the practitioner!) made their own fish with play-dough and cotton bud 'bones'. This enabled the children to use their memories of the fish, their shapes, forms and textures, to reinforce their existing knowledge and develop their design skills. In engaging herself in this provision, the practitioner ensured that the children received support and moved forward, retaining motivation through informed intervention, thus furthering the children's learning. Working across StEPs (as we will see later in the 'Super Cameos' section) allows for progression in any number of aspects and sections for the individual child or collectively for a whole group.

Child development links

Emotionally the children are:

- dealing with likes/dislikes;
- handling the unfamiliar;
- handling different sensations.

Linguistically the children are:

- expressing their thoughts and emotive responses;
- using a range of feelings.

Intellectually the children are:

- responding to the sensory experience;
- reacting to different stimuli.

What links with the Foundation Stage Guidance can be made?

The Personal/Social/Emotional section suggests that children should be:

- interested, excited and motivated to learn;
- confident to try new activities;
- responsive to significant experiences, showing a range of feelings where appropriate.

Within Knowledge and Understanding of the World (K/U of W) children should:

- investigate objects and materials by using their senses as appropriate;
- find out and identify some features of living things;
- look closely at similarities/differences/patterns and change.

Creative Development includes the need for children to:

- respond in a variety of ways to what they see, hear, smell, touch and feel;
- explore texture and shape.

Language and Communication encourages activities enabling children to:

- use talk to clarify ideas and feelings and to interact with interested others;
- extend vocabulary.

ENTITLEMENT 4

Young children are entitled to engage in play experiences that are open-ended and offer trial-and-error learning without fear of failure

CAMEO E4

Context

A group of four children aged $3\frac{1}{2}$–5 years are working in the outdoor play area of a 4+ class. They have decided that they want to cross a grassed area surrounded by tarmac without stepping on the grass. A variety of outdoor resources are available for the children to solve the problem they have set themselves. The practitioner works with the children to decide which resources might be better suited to the job. She then stands back and observes what happens.

Peter (aged 5 years) takes a lead and selects a balancing bar. He drags it to the grass and lays it from the path to the tarmac on the other side. He fetches a wooden support on which to rest the bar and says 'Bring me another one' to whoever happens to be listening. Amy (aged 4 years) picks up a second wooden support and carries it to Peter. Luciano takes the second support and he and Peter fix it to the bar. Rosie looks on at the other three who, by this time, are practising walking – rather tentatively – over the bar. Rosie appears reluctant to attempt this herself.

The practitioner, aware of Rosie's lack of confidence, asks the children if they can find another way of getting across that is less 'scary', as she's not sure she feels confident in going across their construction. The children return to the selection of resources and eventually Peter selects some carpet squares, while Luciano and Amy take some wooden blocks.

Peter places the carpet squares in a line, using each one as a stepping stone in order to lay the next. Then he tells Rosie, 'You get some more, Rosie. We need some more!' Rosie fetches one and walks along the line of carpet squares to take her contribution to Peter, who places it alongside the previous one. Rosie then fetches two more. 'That's it now', Peter says and runs across the carpet to the tarmac. Rosie walks backwards and forwards over the carpet squares looking pleased with herself.

Amy and Luciano place the wooden blocks in a line across the grass. They both try to walk over the line of blocks but find it difficult to balance without stepping off on to the grass. 'You need to make it bigger', shouts Peter and runs to help them retrieve some more blocks. Together they make another row of blocks across the grass and then walk slowly over them. Rosie watches the other three children from the carpet.

The practitioner examines with the children the ideas they have designed to get across the grass. She congratulates them on their achievements and acknowledges their efforts in working together. She discusses their activities with the children and asks them questions about what they might use to solve the problem differently.

What were the children learning?

The children have worked both *individually* and *with others*, including *listening to others' ideas and responding appropriately*. They have demonstrated their *competent use of resources* and have *challenged their physical boundaries* to *extend their capabilities*. They have *recognized a problem* and utilized resources and ideas to *solve it*. They have shown that they are *confident to experiment and accept challenge*, safe in the knowledge that their ideas will be *valued*. They have *communicated their ideas* to each other and talked about the resources that are needed. They have also responded to the practitioner's questions and shown a good knowledge of the *vocabulary* needed for developing their own ideas. Peter in particular has shown *sensitivity* to another child's potential distress.

What is the practitioner's role

The practitioner used her knowledge to support the *children's development as problems-solvers and risk-takers* by providing familiar, safe and *appropriate resources*. She extended the play by *posing a relevant problem* and offering some ideas for a solution. The practitioner gave children *time to plan* their own learning by standing back as an observer, using sensitive teaching intervention only when she noted a situation that may have gone unnoticed by the children. She provided *hands-on* activity using the children's own ideas and environment and gave children the opportunity to *discuss and reflect* on their chosen tasks once it was completed. From her observations she noted particular children's *strengths and weaknesses* and Rosie's insecurity in a physical situation. She will use this knowledge to inform planning for the next stage of the children's learning and note down her impressions of children's development in the setting's records. She will also share this information with her colleagues so that they can assess individual children's responses during similar future activities.

Where to now?

The practitioner uses the children's self-initiated problem-solving to provide other 'problems' in different areas of the class. She encourages the children to talk about their ideas for solving the problems and to test them out in a supportive atmosphere. The children have the opportunity to work together as they try out their ideas. The practitioner can use these activities to develop problem-solving, collaboration and language skills.

Child development links

Physical:

- balances and climbs (4-year-old);
- is agile, energetic, flexible in movement (5-year-old).

Intellectual:

- spends time wondering about things (3-year-old);
- develops ideas about basic measurement, more, bigger, enough (4-year-old);
- concentrates for 7 minutes (5-year-old).

Linguistic:

- uses vocabulary for requests, questions, tells about (4-year-old);
- has different language from adult – differs in style rather than grammar (4-year-old).

What links with the Foundation Stage Guidance can be made?

Personal/Social/Emotional:

- Rosie understands that what she does can affect someone else's emotions;
- she gained personal satisfaction from being trusted to carry out tasks.

In general the children showed themselves to be:

- confident to try new activities, initiate ideas and speak in a familiar group;
- able to form good relationships with adults and peers;

- able to work as part of a group or class;
- able to select and use activities and resources independently.

Physical Development includes children's ability to:

- move with confidence, imagination and in safety;
- move with control and coordination;
- show awareness of space of themselves and of others.

Creative Development includes the need for children to:

- express and communicate their ideas clearly.

Within K/U of W, the children were able to:

- build and construct a wide range of objects, selecting appropriate resources and adapting their work where necessary.

In terms of Language and Communication, the children:

- were able to speak in a familiar group situation;
- used talk to organize, sequence and clarify thinking and ideas;
- interacted with others, negotiating plans and activities;
- spoke clearly and audibly with confidence and control and showed awareness of the listener.

Mathematically the children could:

- use language such as 'more' or 'less' in practical activities;
- discuss and begin to use the vocabulary involved in adding.

ENTITLEMENT 5

Young children are entitled to playful, exploratory and experiential activities with a variety of materials and resources and within a variety of contexts

CAMEO E5

Context

A Year 2 class has been thinking about the effects of weather and, in particular, as it is winter, the effects of freezing. The children have explored the changing structure of water as it freezes and have also had a range of experiences outdoors at testing temperatures and observing frosty surfaces in sunny and shady spots. On this particular day, ice blocks of varying sizes have been placed by the teacher in the water tray; some include a 'surprise', as we shall see.

The activity provided involves a group of three children: Lauren, Jamie and Emma. Emma, a wheelchair user, is a quiet, self-confident child with a good grasp on most learning situations, but she is often a silent observer. She does, however, find problem-solving stimulating and challenging.

Lauren shouts across, 'Look in here. It's ice!' Lauren proceeds to manipulate the ice shapes and is joined by Emma and Jamie. Lauren rolls up her sleeves and puts both hands into the tray, lifting out a large block of solid ice.

Lauren: Ooooh – feel this Emma, it's really heavy.

Emma watches without participating but remains focused on Lauren and Jamie. Lauren lifts a block of ice and holds it close to her cheek. She then breathes heavily on to the ice and moves it to inspect it more closely. She turns to Emma.

Lauren: Look. This bit's clear and this bit's white.

Lauren rubs the ice with her fingers and comments on its 'smoothness' and density.

Jamie: Look. It's frozen hard.

Lauren notices a leaf trapped in a piece of ice and asks Emma to examine it. Lauren begins to scratch the surface of the ice with her fingers to no avail. Emma looks around, finds a box with some selected implements in it and picks up a fork. She begins to scrape and stab the fork into the ice. Lauren immediately finds a fork and copies. Jamie leans over and decides that, if they want to get at the leaf, 'You've got to melt it'. Lauren moves close to the ice and breathes on it again.

Emma: No, don't do that. I know what to do. Water. My dad uses a kettle on the car when it's frosty.
Lauren: We need some hot water.

Jamie seeks out the teacher and asks for some hot water. He then takes the jug to the others and asks, 'Why do you need hot water?'

Lauren: We can see a leaf in here and we need to get it out.
Emma: . . . to melt it.

The teacher joins the group while Lauren pours water on to the ice block. As it thaws, all the children have gathered round to watch as Lauren, smiling, gently pulls out the leaf.

What were the children learning?

The ice activity is part of the Science curriculum in KS1: scientific exploration and investigation. The children explore using *their senses* and are learning to *distinguish the different characteristics and properties* of ice. *Working individually and in pairs* the children investigate *cause and effect*, showing sustained concentration and perseverance. They are able to *use appropriate language to express familiar and new experiences.*

What was the practitioner's role?

The teacher made provision for limited – but not limiting – resources, which had been *carefully conceived* to provide opportunities for *children to build on prior knowledge* and *progress* to the next stage in their *understanding of the effects* of heat on ice. By providing the large blocks of ice (one with a 'surprise' inclusion) and a *range of possible tools* nearby, *exploration and experimentation* were promoted. The teacher allowed *time* for the children to *interact and engage with the learning environment*. He unobtrusively *observed* the children during the initial stages of the activity to *assess* their understanding and existing knowledge so that appropriate *adult intervention and support* could be given when relevant. This teaching approach, rather than an interventionist one, encouraged children to *hypothesize, predict* and *make their own thinking and understanding overt.*

Where to now?

The workshop session concludes with the opportunity for each group of children who have been engaged with the ice sharing with class members their experiences and discoveries; needless to say, Lauren proudly sports the leaf she has 'found'. The activity generated much excitement from everyone and included new learning, reinforcement of existing knowledge, and a playful basis upon which to develop scientific concepts and vocabulary. The teacher also enjoyed the opportunity to see the results of children's previous experiences with ice and was delighted when the children requested more similar activities. His planning for continuity and progression in the following week included other materials that melt and thaw. The whole class was involved in putting ice in different locations and predicting what would happen under the different conditions.

Child development links

Because Emma is in a wheelchair it is sometimes more difficult for her to have 'hands-on' play experiences. The adult and the other children, however, capitalize on her mental abilities and value her contribution. The Child Development charts show intellectual development at the level of a 6-year-old, in that the child 'begins to take interest in the wider world' and to 'show understanding of abstract ideas'. At the 7-year-old level, the child 'asks questions about cause and effect', 'enjoys the challenge of experimenting with new materials' and 'uses reversible thought operations to change opinion'.

What links with KS1 can be made?

In Science, the children showed themselves able to:

SC1 (2a) ask questions and decide how they might find answers to them;
(2b) use first-hand experience and simple information sources to answer questions;
(2c) think about what might happen before deciding what to do;
(2i) compare what happened with what they expected would happen and try to explain it, drawing on their knowledge and understanding;
(2j) review their work and explain what they did to others.
SC3 (1b) sort objects into groups on the basis of simple material properties;
(2b) explore and describe the way some everyday materials change when they are cooled.

ENTITLEMENT 6

Young children are entitled to engage in individual and dynamic play and learning experiences relevant to their age group and stage of development

CAMEO 6.1

Context

The children in a Year 2 class have been thinking about boats as part of a science theme on floating and sinking. The children have designed and made boats using 'found' materials of their own choice and one child, George (aged nearly 7 years), is really keen to test his boat to see if it will float. In a plenary session, the teacher encourages the children to discuss their designs and to begin to make predictions and hypotheses as to which boat is likely to float most successfully and what constitutes a 'good' boat. The teacher, Anne, scribes some of the children's ideas as an example of recording for a specific purpose. The following day, Anne overhears one parent talking to another about a 'boat race'. It appears that the children have been talking widely about the possibility of testing their boats, prompted by George.

During a discussion session that morning, the teacher takes up the issue of finding a venue for such a boat race. Various suggestions are made by the children: the water tray, the river, the lake near the school, a paddling pool, the school swimming pool. Children are asked to suggest arguments for and against each proposal on a list written up on the board. The final consensus is that the swimming pool is the best place. Two children write a letter to the Head seeking permission to use the pool and the teacher agreed to check necessary safety issues. The children then begin to plan how the race will take place.

A free period for the swimming pool is found on Wednesday of the following week, which means that the children have only 5 school days to refine their models. All the children make one boat with several (including George) making two. Many of the children use reference books and the internet to try to identify appropriate boat shapes and materials. Children spend a great deal of time discussing and arguing about their designs and every bit of time outside 'set' curriculum areas is given over to trialling and testing different materials and resources.

After the race the children are given the opportunity to write a journalistic report (literacy: shared writing) about the race, which will be published in the school newspaper.

What were the children learning?

The children were *exploring and challenging* themselves as well as *cooperating and collaborating with adults and peers*. They showed great *respect for others' views and ideas* and an ability to *judge and estimate* mathematically and scientifically. They were able to *share experiences and interests*, *make effective choices* and use a range of *reasoning skills*. They were able to expand significantly their *use of vocabulary* related to sinking, floating and experimentation and were able to *accept failure* and use it as a stepping stone to progression. In writing their accounts of the boat race, they were able to *write in a different genre* and for a different *audience*, and *share the process of writing* with others.

What is the practitioner's role?

Anne was able to *support and extend the children's thinking* through the opportunities and *range of resources* provided. Her *meticulous planning* of the event, and the time she gave the children to *explore their own ideas* and to *make informed choices*, meant that the children were engaged and motivated and her time could be spent in *observing and extending* individuals' learning. Anne *responded to the children's views* so that she was able to *incorporate their spontaneous activity* into her teaching and to *capitalize on individual interests* to *extend learning* for all the children. She *challenged their existing knowledge and skills* and *enabled them to review, reinforce and validate* their own ideas.

Where to now?

The practitioner could expand on the interest of the children in the topic (boats) by encouraging them to use the skills they have learned in investigating and researching into other related topics. Through her teaching, she could show the children the different ways of constructing and using different tools (e.g. wood, clay). She should encourage them to estimate about the boat race: How long will the boats take to cross the water? How will they measure the length of time (links to mathematics)?

Child development links:

Social:

- as 7-year-olds, the children prefer more detail in their activities and so demand accuracy in their play props: this enhances their concentration and level of interest in their boats.

Physical:

- because they are more skilled in their fine manipulative skills, children are able to make their boats more realistic.

Intellectual:

- children are open to challenge and experiment with new materials;
- they develop both mathematical and scientific concepts;
- they accept the challenge of exploring topics independently through books, television programmes and computers;
- they formulate plans and strategies.

Linguistic:

- 7-year-olds are capable of reasoning with others logically;
- they use appropriate language, including internal speech.

What links with KS1 can be made?

SCIENCE Unit 2D – grouping and changing materials: planning experimental work.
Opportunities were given for children to:

- suggest ideas and solutions based on simple knowledge and to say how they might find out about them;
- offer ideas on what they think might happen in an experiment;
- think about and discuss whether comparisons or tests are fair/unfair;
- compare everyday materials and objects on the basis of their material properties, including hardness, strength, flexibility, and relate these properties to everyday uses of materials.

ENGLISH En 3 – Writing. Children were able to:

(1b) sequence events and recount them in appropriate detail;

(1e) vary their writing to suit the purpose and reader (teachers, other children);

(2d) write extended texts with support;

(5h) understand the importance of clear and neat presentation to communicate their meaning effectively.

PLAYING, LEARNING AND TEACHING ACROSS THE ENTITLEMENTS

The preceding cameos illustrate aspects of single Entitlements. However, children's play and learning is usually much wider and often does not fall into tidy categories. The following 'super' cameo shows children and practitioners playing and learning across StEPs. Using the Pack, including the Child Development Charts, and her knowledge of the curriculum, this practitioner (Pat) is able to make secure and significant links between the children's prior knowledge, different aspects of their development and link these with aspects that will move them forward in their learning. To do this, she uses her teaching experience and prior pedagogic knowledge to provide relevant resources and to teach at a level matching the children's stage of learning and development, as you will see.

SUPER CAMEO

It is autumn and the 3-year-old children have been bringing in leaves they have found on the way to the playgroup. The practitioners have decided to focus on autumn as a theme for 4 weeks. As part of this they take the children to the local park to give them experience of seeing the leaves fall from the trees.

Bibi, Julian and Sara are holding their buckets carefully as they enter the park. At the side of the path are piles of fallen leaves. The practitioner scrunches the leaves underfoot and the children join in, laughing. Julian bends down to look at a leaf, then picks it up. 'This one's a big leaf, a giant, a giant leaf!' he exclaims. The others start to search for big leaves and save the best in their buckets. 'I've got a teeny, tiny one – the baby!' says Sara.

The whole group sit under the tall trees to eat sandwiches they have made earlier for the visit. They watch the leaves being blown off the trees and falling all around them.

Julian tells everyone about the hedgehog that comes into his garden and recalls what his mother has told him about hedgehogs making nests out of leaves. Bibi is picking gently through the leaves in her bucket – 'a green one, a brown one . . . two brown ones'.

Next day at Playgroup, the practitioner shares a book about hedgehogs with the children at the dough table and Julian makes a hedgehog, using twigs for prickles. The others watch and do the same. He then takes the hedgehog to the pile of leaves on the table and the children play with their hedgehogs making nests for them. Sara makes a dough tree with real leaves and 'blows' them down for the hedgehogs.

Practitioner's role

The practitioner decided to use the children's interest in the fallen leaves to start a new topic linking with the time of year. She knows that most of the children live in maisonettes with no gardens, so she takes them to the local park to observe the trees and leaves. At the park, the practitioner leads the children in exploring and collecting. She gives the children as much direct experience of where the fallen leaves come from as possible by sitting the children under the trees for their picnic and observing the effects of the wind.

The following day, the practitioner had brought with her a book to follow-up Julian's interest and to use this to increase the knowledge of the other children. Having provided dough, twigs, straws and lollipop sticks, it is possible for the children to extend their model-making into imaginative play as the table of things collected at the park is for the children to touch, handle and use rather than just to look at.

Whilst planned against Entitlement 1 – 'Young children are entitled to play experiences which engage them affectively and socially in their own and other's learning' – the following links show clearly how it is possible to include a number of other Entitlements in one learning experience for the children.

What were the children learning?

Entitlement 2:
By going to the park the children were having an experience that was *relevant* to their current interests and was, therefore, a *meaningful context*. They were able to *talk about and share their life experiences*. They showed *confidence in their own abilities with familiar equipment* when they used the dough for their own purposes and *persevered and concentrated on the tasks*.

Entitlement 3:
The children were able to show their *curiosity* in their natural surroundings in the park and to use this *imaginatively and creatively* the next day. The children were encouraged to *explore and respond to sensory experiences* in the park and were clear about the *contrast between fantasy and reality* in their role play.

Entitlement 4:
These activities were *open-ended* and allowed the children to *collaborate and cooperate, participating in small social groups*. They were *consolidating and extending their knowledge of the world*. Julian's ideas were *valued* and used to *extend the children's capabilities*.

Entitlement 5:
The leaves activity is playful, exploratory and constitutes an essential experience for children with a variety of materials and resources such as leaves, dough, twigs and such like, and within the context of both the playgroup and the park.

Entitlement 6:
In all of the above, the children were learning to *share ideas, experiences and interests*. They made their own discoveries, gaining *emotional security through being valued and respected*.

What is the practitioner's role?

Entitlement 2:
The practitioners have an understanding of *what is meaningful and relevant in children's lives*. They are *building on children's prior knowledge* by arranging a visit to a *learning environment that reflects children's starting points, and features of the area in which they live*.

Entitlement 3:
The practitioners were making it possible for the children to *collaborate and play alongside peers and adults*. The children's *own responses were valued* and allowed opportunities for them *to initiate ideas within groups*.

Entitlement 4:
The practitioner was aware of what *resources are appropriate to support children's learning* and showed *flexibility within a framework* both by going out of the setting and by allowing free use of the resources in

the room. The practitioner had *time to listen* and was ready to *participate in discussions*.

Entitlement 5:
The range of resources provided by the practitioner, being relatively 'limited' to the focus, enabled the children to focus on the playful aspect of the activity and to explore and experiment in the context of sensitive adult support.

Entitlement 6:
By taking all the children to the park in small groups, the practitioner allowed *all children to engage in activities*. She provided *developmentally appropriate resources* and *valued the contributions made* by the children. By giving appropriate experiences to the children and *valuing their contribution*, she provided them with a *positive self-image*.

Links to child development

Social – 3-year-olds:

- responds positively if conditions are favourable;
- engages in parallel and associative play;
- is cooperative in actions and likes to please adults.

Cognitive – 3-year-olds:

- concentrates for 5 minutes.

Cognitive – 4-year-olds:

- distinguishes different characteristics of objects through texture, shape and colour.

Language – 3-year-olds:

- starts/stops flow of speech, needs to gather thoughts to express something for which she does not have words;
- talks about past experiences.

Links with the Foundation Stage Guidance

The goals towards which these 3-year-old children are working are:

Personal/Social/Emotional:

- continue to be interested, excited and motivated to learn;
- be confident to try new activities, initiate ideas and speak in a familiar group;
- maintain attention, concentrate;
- select and use activities and resources independently.

Language and Literacy:

- use talk to organize, sequence and clarify thinking, ideas, feelings and events;
- sustain attentive listening, responding to what they have heard by relevant comments, questions or actions.

Mathematics:

- use language to compare two numbers or quantities.

Knowledge and Understanding of the World:

- investigate objects and materials by using all of their senses as appropriate;
- find out about and identify some features of living things, objects and events they observe;
- build and construct with a wide range of objects, selecting appropriate resources, and adapting their work where necessary;
- observe, find out about and identify features in the place they live and the natural world.

Creative:

- explore colour, texture, shape, form and space in two and three dimensions;
- respond in a variety of ways to what they see, hear, smell, touch and feel;
- express and communicate their ideas, thoughts and feelings by using a widening range of materials . . . imaginative and role-play.

In the hands of quality practitioners, the StEPs Pack is clearly flexible and capable of being used to great effect to support young children's development and learning.

FINALE

We hope you will enjoy using the Pack as much as we have enjoyed working together to develop it. What we also hope is that you will find unique and different ways to extend and expand the Pack for your own uses. There is one proviso, of course. Do ensure that whatever you do is playful and progressive both for the children and for you. That way, you will enjoy each other's company and continue to learn in ways most appropriate to early childhood education.

SECTION EIGHT

Child development charts

Chart 1: Social development 3-7 years

	In the context of social development, the average 3-year-old:	In the context of social development, the average 4-year-old:	In the context of social development, the average 5-year-old:	In the context of social development, the average 6-year-old:	In the context of social development, the average 7-year-old:
Ability to relate to others	responds positively if conditions are favourable, e.g. space, materials, etc. forms first friendships	can expand sense of self through boasts and brags offers things to others and wants to please friends	can be easily discouraged or encouraged can cooperate individually to achieve group goal	begins to recognize that not all people have the same opinions finds friendships may be disrupted by differences in opinion	develops mature friendship relationships is serious, absorbed and sympathetic to others
One to one child	engages in parallel and associative play; looks in from sidelines; works separately but plays next to peers	begins interactive play but, as yet, finds difficulty taking turns	understands power of rejecting others, e.g. 'I'm not your friend'	expresses preferences	is less domineering and less set on having own way
One to many children	can begin to resolve many social situations but needs help if conflict occurs	lacks verbal skills to resolve conflicts becomes angry easily if events are not going their way	uses verbal rather than physical aggression shares fantasies to make friends	cheats to win a game can be unsure as to whom to ask for help	takes more prevalent risks develops sophisticated social skills
One to one adult	is cooperative in actions and likes to please adults has some difficulty taking turns and sharing	self-regulates; expected behaviour increases but needs to be reminded begins to justify negative acts, e.g. 'He hit me first'	is not as dependent upon adults to solve conflicts likes to conform and please adults lies rather than admits to not following rules	is keen on getting her or his own way in group situation is interested in good or bad behaviour of others	questions ground rules, especially if adult is seen to break them has an internal standard of goodness and sense of fair play
Member of complex social system	becomes more interested in own environment increases awareness of social roles; role-taking becomes part of play elaborates pretence play with objects understands only a little about how easily animals and plants can be harmed identifies and labels own and others' sex	becomes more interested in other children than in adults uses pretence to strengthen social/emotional skills, etc. uses, for example, a puppet or doll to become an actor in sequenced themes takes on a host of pretend characters uses substitutes in play props, e.g. block for telephone has special friends, usually of same sex	engages in pretend play to help overcome fears uses imagination to transport him or herself from home to somewhere imaginary, e.g. a forest knows sexual stability – that they are, were and will be a girl or boy	plays at a higher level of social collaboration develops more stage-managed and scripted play	engages in collaborative pretence as more important for building trust prefers more detail and accuracy in play props understands gender constancy – boys and girls remain the same regardless of clothes, situation, etc.

CHILD DEVELOPMENT CHARTS

	In the context of physical development, the average 3-year-old:	In the context of physical development, the average 4-year-old:	In the context of physical development, the average 5-year-old:	In the context of physical development, the average 6-year-old:	In the context of physical development, the average 7-year-old:
Gross motor skills	runs, jumps, walks on tiptoe runs and stops with increasing control rolls sideways, curls up small kicks ball stands still becomes adept at climbing jumps with two feet together from low height improves manoeuvring skills, e.g. on foot tricycle balances on one foot walks alone upstairs two feet to step is primarily interested in manipulation of materials rather than creation of object paints with large strokes cuts out simple shapes	balances on different parts of the body makes whole–part body responses to music, e.g. clap, stamp rolls head over heels moves at contrasting speeds kicks ball when running climbs ladders, trees, nets hangs from bar by knees runs on tiptoe hops forwards is more confident with running and jumping rather than catching and hitting throws ball overhand walks up and down steps, one foot per step holds pencil with pincer grasp	has complete binocular vision runs and climbs with confidence skips with feet is agile, energetic, flexible in movement stops immediately on cue begins to move on to bicycle throws ball more easily than catches catches using whole arm counts fingers on one hand with index finger develops left/right hand preference copies or writes own name independently but some reversals likely copies square, triangle threads large needle, sews large stitches	is aware of own body and self-control leads and follows patterns and sequences learns to use skipping rope judges/estimates distance, direction and height understands and uses contrasting strength rides two-wheel bike uses bat adequately begins to use hands to catch ball throws/catches smaller ball forms letters correctly and ability is building; some reversals may still occur	develops balance, e.g. walk along narrow width roller skates, swims, dives, etc., with confidence becomes more experimental varies speed with activities manages bat and ball in team games coordinates hand/eye in bat/ball games and growth is evident forms readable print; attempts to make writing smaller; reversals rarer produces more detailed drawings sews, threads needles with ease enjoys making models that result in detailed realistic production; attends to detail using manipulative skills
Fine motor skills	scribbles freely, copies O (closed shapes) or X paints and draws more recognizable figures/outlines draws people with basic head and extremities grasps pencil with whole hand combines visual and manipulative skills, e.g. completes simple jigsaw builds tower of up to nine bricks	has greater fine motor control with pencil draws simple house copies simple shapes threads small beads but not usually needles forms flat cakes, balls, narrow strips of clay builds tower of more than ten cubes	pours from container – this becomes more reliable	grasps pencil and adjusts pencil to gain better control builds complex arrangement of bricks	enjoys building blocks that have complex interlocking pieces

	In the context of emotional development/ independence, the average 3-year-old:	In the context of emotional development/ independence, the average 4-year-old:	In the context of emotional development/ independence, the average 5-year-old:	In the context of emotional development/ independence, the average 6-year-old:	In the context of emotional development/ independence, the average 7-year-old:
Emotional	expresses intense feelings – fear, affection; has silly sense of humour is egocentric: 'Who am I? What makes me?' throws things/hits when upset adds his or her opinion to general discussion develops an understanding between behaviour and others' understanding of that behaviour is able to make free choices; learns control, also shame, if something is not handled correctly has a sense of morality affected by good/bad activities and how they are handled eats with fork and spoon manages and enjoys different roles, e.g. fetching, tidying up follows basic hygiene of washing, brushing hair	controls intense fear/anger with greater ability; still needs adult help to express and control feelings has a developing sense of identity/ name and where he or she belongs in wider community understands that what he or she does can affect someone else's emotions has less visible attachment behaviour; does not seek assurance from carer as frequently is more assertive and aggressive in social groups sometimes dresses and feeds self unaided eats skilfully with spoon and fork comforts another child in distress goes to the toilet unaided understands taking turns	enjoys others and behaves in warm empathetic manner has positive view of self-worth; behaviour reflects view of self jokes, teases to gain attention is tender and protective towards younger children/ pets cooperates, understands rules and fair play has sense of morality affected by group norms, laws, etc. gains personal satisfaction from being trusted to carry out tasks dresses and feeds self but needs help with cutting meat uses knife and fork helps to do fastenings when dressing washes her or himself	asks 'what sort of person am I?' Begins to develop opinion formed by own feelings enjoys looking after younger children but still needs supervision from adult models behaviour on adults he or she respects understands and manipulates emotions, e.g. 'I won't cry or they'll laugh at me' enjoys choosing clothes to wear has physical skills to serve out food learns about adult expectations at the table begins to tie shoelaces	questions 'What sort of person am I?' by listening to opinions of others; uses measurements he or she accepts as important develops global evaluation of themselves; discrepancy between what he or she would like to be and what he or she thinks of self – the narrower the gap the higher the self-esteem can use verbal skills to demonstrate aggression has a sense of morality effected by social contracts, ethical principles begins to make independent decisions about what is right and wrong does not find it easy to comfort someone in distress has absorbed basic cultural skills and norms ties shoelaces with confidence
Responsibility	is distracted by absorbing play can carry simple verbal messages understands sharing		enjoys making decisions and being involved in planning		bathes self with little adult supervision speaks up for self, e.g. at the dentist or doctors

CHILD DEVELOPMENT CHARTS

	In the context of cognitive development, the average 3-year-old:	In the context of cognitive development, the average 4-year-old:	In the context of cognitive development, the average 5-year-old:	In the context of cognitive development, the average 6-year-old:	In the context of cognitive development, the average 7-year-old:
Thought	has the urge to ask 'Why?'; spends time wondering about things decides when to start/stop an activity has marked development in listening skills assumes everyone knows and experiences the world in the same way as self; uses the phase 'I know' concentrates for 5 minutes matches 2–3 primary colours is interested in numbers; enjoys counting real objects finds it difficult to view something from another person's perspective; states what is seen	understands there are many worlds and that other people know and experience things differently understands that people think but does not understand they can be thinking about their thinking becomes aware of concepts like near/far, hot/cold concentrates for 6 minutes matches and names 4 primary colours counts up to at least 10 items learns many number names and their ordering develops ideas about basic measurement, e.g. big, little enjoys naming and classifying world around them	progresses to 'You know that I know' concentrates for 7 minutes names 4 primary colours; matches 10–12 colours counts up to at least 20 items recognizes simple shapes	begins to take interest in wider world around them, e.g. other countries, past concentrates for 8 minutes becomes more confident in recognizing and writing numbers recognizes properties of shape develops relationship between clock time and daily events	asks questions about cause and effect explores using language skills enjoys challenge of experimenting with new materials understands that her or his own thinking and that of others occurs continually and follows certain rules concentrates for 9 minutes develops concepts of mathematical and scientific understanding carries out simple mental calculations has some understanding of money and giving change explores topics independently through books, TV programmes
Learning	appreciates time; differences between past and present confuses fact and fiction	carries a tune, recognizes melody, sings short simple songs	begins to distinguish different levels of size/measurement, e.g. thin/fat, tall/short	reads simple music notation; plays simple tunes	uses reversible thought operations to change opinion
Understanding		distinguishes different characteristics of objects through texture, shape and colour compares different looking objects does not draw representations of objects overlapping plays games with a few simple rules and uses a simple scoring system; enjoys games that rely on chance	learns that print communicates meaning classifies larger groups, e.g. cats, dogs has interest in a specific topic; may show detailed knowledge enjoys playing and planning miniature worlds	begins to learn more about needs of plants and animals begins to show understanding of abstract ideas	formulates plans and strategies when playing games

	In the context of language development, the average 3-year-old:	**In the context of language development, the average 4-year-old:**	**In the context of language development, the average 5-year-old:**	**In the context of language development, the average 6-year-old:**	**In the context of language development, the average 7-year-old:**
Speaking/ understanding	uses spoken language and has learned to fill in with gestures starts/stops flow of speech; needs to gather thoughts to express something for which he or she does not have words uses past tense of words by adding ed, e.g. holded, goed has vocabulary of around 1000+ words takes ideas literally, e.g. 'frog in the throat' gives full name and sex talks about past experience	uses vocabulary for requests, questions, tells about, argues, etc. holds simple turn-taking conversation has different language from adult – differs in style rather than grammar uses language skills in imaginative play gives age and home address	gets pleasure from playing with language, e.g. varying voice expresses feelings through talk is aware of language spoken in different ways has fluent, grammatical speech has vocabulary of several thousand words begins to give definitions in words and shares grasp of the abstract ceases to take sayings literally, e.g. no real frog in throat begins to talk about past, future and present	listens to others talk and understands their feelings accurately produces local accent, family accent; learns to move between two holds long conversations with another child or adult, involving listening and turn-taking pronounces majority of sounds from their language often asks for meaning of unknown words uses language to describe, questions, guesses, explains, justifies, complains is more confident with past-tense verbs, e.g. held, went, etc.	knows cultural procedure for talking to different people, e.g. peers, adults, teachers enjoys gossip and chats with other children he or she would not wish to share with an adult is ready to sort out acting from reality, e.g. on television has sense of genres for talk, e.g. telling jokes, etc. reasons logically with use of language, including internal speech and thinking out loud plans, speculates, thinks ahead
Reading/ writing	*Writing* makes marks on paper; Concentrates on controlling pencil rather than communicating message *Reading* enjoys listening to stories/looking at pictures themselves prefers realistic, credible stories	*Writing* experiments with marks on paper; intention of communicating message or emulating adult writing begins to form and recognize different language symbols *Reading* displays reading-like behaviours; reconstructs stories for themselves shows natural interest in books and language of print has difficulty distinguishing between b and d enjoys wild, dramatic, fantasy stories	*Writing* is aware that speech can be written down *Reading* uses memory of familiar texts to match some spoken or written words realizes print contains constant message comments on pictures but seldom questions text	*Writing* begins to consider audience when writing finds difficulty dealing with two elements of writing at once, e.g. spelling and punctuation *Reading* reads unfamiliar texts slowly; focuses on reading exactly what is on the page; begins to use strategies to sort out unknown words prefers stories about fears, magic, nature and the elements	*Writing* is aware that languages are written in different ways using different alphabets controls punctuation and spelling depending on complexity of task is familiar with most aspects of the writing process *Reading* integrates a variety of reading strategies adapts reading to different types of text with teacher support, can comment on or criticize text uses contents and index in books enjoys both fiction and non-fiction books, newspapers, comics, magazines

REFERENCES

Adams, S. (2000) An investigation of the deconstruction and reconstruction processes within the context of reflective pedagogical practice and with the content of play. PhD thesis, University of Leicester School of Education.

Adams, S. and Moyles, J. (2000) Giant StEPs or small strides? Developing early years curriculum provision through reflective practice. Paper presented at ECER Conference, Edinburgh, September.

Adams, S., Medland, P. and Moyles, J. (2000) Supporting play-based teaching through collaborative practice-based research. *Support for Learning*, 15(4), 15–64.

Anning, A. and Edwards, A. (1999) *Promoting Children's Learning 3 to 5: The New Early Years Professional*. Buckingham: Open University Press.

Athey, C. (1994) *Extending Thought in Young Children*. London: Paul Chapman.

Barnardos (1995) *Playing it Safe*. London: Barnardos Publications.

Beetlestone, F. (1998) *Creative Children: Imaginative Teaching*. Buckingham: Open University Press.

Bennett, N., Wood, E. and Rogers, S. (1997) *Teaching Through Play: Teachers' Thinking and Classroom Practice*. Buckingham: Open University Press.

Bilton, H. (1998) *Outdoor Play in the Early Years*. London: David Fulton.

Birmingham City Council/NFER-Nelson (1997) *Signposts: Baseline Assessment for the Primary Phase*. Birmingham/Windsor: BCC/NFER-Nelson.

Blakemore, C. (2000) *Gender and Society: The Herbert Spencer Lectures*. Oxford: Oxford University Press.

Blenkin, G. and Kelly, A. (1997) *Principles into Practice in Early Childhood Education*. London: Paul Chapman.

Bredekamp, S. (ed.) (1987) *Developmentally Appropriate Practice in Early Childhood Programs Serving Children from Birth Through Age 8*. Washington, DC: National Association for the Education of Young Children.

Bruce, T. (1998) *Supporting Play in the Early Years*. London: Hodder & Stoughton.

Claxton, G. (1998) *Hare Brain: Tortoise Mind: Why Intelligence Increases When You Think Less*. London: Fourth Estate.

Cook, H. and Finlayson, H. (1999) *Interactive Children: Communicative Teaching*. Buckingham: Open University Press.

Curtis, A. (1998) *A Curriculum for the Pre-school Child: Learning to Learn*, 2nd edn. London: Routledge.

de Boo, M. (1999) *Enquiring Children, Challenging Teaching*. Buckingham: Open University Press.

Department for Education and Employment (1999) *All Our Futures: Creativity, Culture and Education*. Report to the Secretary of State for Education and Employment. London: National Advisory Committee on Creative and Cultural Education.

Donaldson, M. (1992) *Human Minds*. Glasgow: Fontana.

Duffy, B. (1998) *Supporting Creativity and Imagination in the Early Years*. Buckingham: Open University Press.

Early Childhood Education Forum/National Children's Bureau (ECEF/NCB) (1998) *Quality in Diversity in Early Learning*. London: National Children's Bureau.

Early Years Curriculum Group (1998) *Interpreting the National Curriculum at KS1*. Buckingham: Open University Press.

Edwards, A. and Knight, P. (1994) *Effective Early Years Education*. Buckingham: Open University Press.

Elkind, D. (1988) *The Hurried Child: Growing Up Too Fast Too Soon*, 2nd edn. Reading, MA: Addison Wesley.

Fisher, J. (1996) *Starting from the Child? Teaching and Learning from 4–8*. Buckingham: Open University Press.

Galton, M., Hargreaves, L., Comber, C., Wall, D. and Pell, T. (1999) *Inside the Primary Classroom: Twenty Years On*. London: Routledge.

Goleman, D. (1996) *Emotional Intelligence. Why it Can Matter More than IQ*. London: Bloomsbury.

Healy, J. (1998) *Failure to Connect: How Computers Affect our Children's Minds – for Better and Worse*. New York: Simon & Schuster.

Hurst, V. and Joseph, J. (1998) *Supporting Early Learning: The Way Forward*. Buckingham: Open University Press.

Hutchin, V. (1996) *Tracking Significant Achievement in the Early Years*. London: Hodder & Stoughton.

Katz, L. (1995) *Talks with Teachers of Young Children*. Norwood, NJ: Ablex.

Kotulak, R. (1996) *Inside the Brain: Revolutionary Discoveries of How the Mind Works*. Kansas City, MO: Andrews & McMeel.

Kozulin, (1998) *Psychological Tools: A Sociocultural Approach to Education*. Cambridge, MA: Harvard University Press.

Lindon, J. (1993) *Child Development from Birth to Eight: A Practical Focus*. London: National Children's Bureau.

Maude, P. (2001) *Physical Children: Active Teaching*. Buckingham: Open University Press.

Merry, R. (1997) Children's development 7–11. In Kitson, N. and Merry, R. (eds), *Teaching in the Primary School: The Learning Relationship*. London: Routledge.

Merry, R. (1998) *Successful Children: Successful Teaching*. Buckingham: Open University Press.

Moriarty, V. and Siraj-Blatchford, I. (1998) *An Introduction to Curriculum for 3–5 year-olds*. Nottingham: Education Now.

Moyles, J. (1989) *Just Playing? The Role and Status of Play in Early Childhood Education*. Milton Keynes: Open University Press.

Moyles, J.R. (ed.) (1994) *The Excellence of Play*. Buckingham: Open University Press.

Moyles, J. (2001) *Playful Children: Inspired Teaching*. Buckingham: Open University Press.

Moyles, J. and Adams, S. (2000) A tale of the unexpected: practitioners' expectations and children's play. *Journal of In-service Education*, 26(2), 349–69.

Moyles, J. and Suschitzky, W. (1998a) Painting the cabbages red? Training for support staff in early years classrooms. In Abbott, L. and Pugh, G. (eds), *Training Issues in the Early Years*. Buckingham: Open University Press.

Moyles, J. and Suschitzky, W. (1998b) *Teaching Fledglings to Fly: Mentoring in the Primary School*. London: The Association of Teachers and Lecturers/University of Leicester.

Norway Royal Ministry of Church, Education and Research (1994) *Core Curriculum for Primary, Secondary and Adult Education in Norway*. Oslo: NRMCER.

Nutbrown, C. (ed.) (1996) *Children's Rights and Early Education*. London: Paul Chapman.

OHMCI (1999) *Standards and Quality in the Early Years*. Cardiff: OHMCI.

Parliamentary Office of Science and Technology (2000) *Early Years Learning (Post 140)*. June, London. http://www.parliament.uk/post/home/htm

Pascal, C. and Bertram, A. (1997) *Effective Early Learning: Case Studies in Improvement*. London: Hodder & Stoughton.

Qualifications and Curriculum Authority (1997) *Baseline Assessment Scales*. London: School Curriculum and Assessment Authority.

Qualifications and Curriculum Authority (2000a) *Early Learning Goals*. London: DfEE.

Qualifications and Curriculum Authority (2000b) *Curriculum Guidance for the Foundation Stage*. London: DfEE.

Qualifications and Curriculum Authority (2000c) *The National Curriculum: Handbook for Primary Teachers in England, Key Stages 1 and 2*. London: DfEE/QCA.

Roberts, R. (1995) *Self-esteem and Successful Early Learning*. London: Hodder & Stoughton.

Sayeed, Z. and Guerin, E. (2000) *Early Years Play: A Happy Medium for Assessment and Intervention*. London: David Fulton.

Scottish Education Department (1995) *Curriculum 5–14*. Edinburgh: SED.

Scottish Education Department (1999) *Pre-school Educational Research: Linking Policy with Practice*. Report edited by Valerie Wilson and Jane Ogden-Smith. Edinburgh: The Stationery Office.

Siraj-Blatchford, I. (1999) *A Curriculum Development Handbook for Early Childhood Educators*. Stoke-on-Trent: Trentham Books.

Siraj-Blatchford, I. and Clarke, P. (2000) *Supporting Identity, Diversity and Language in the Early Years*. Buckingham: Open University Press.

Smilansky, S. (1968) *The Effects of the Socio-Dramatic Play on Disadvantaged Children*. New York: John Wiley.

Smilansky, S. and Shefatya, L. (1990) *Facilitating Play: A Medium for Promoting Cognitive Socio-Emotional and Academic Development in Young Children*. Gaithersburg, MD: Psychosocial and Educational Publications.

Suschitzky, W. and Chapman, J. (1998) *Valued Children: Informed Teaching*. Buckingham: Open University Press.

Sutton-Smith, B. (1998) *The Ambiguity of Play*. Cambridge, MA: Harvard University Press.

Webb, L. (1974) *Purpose and Practice in Nursery Education*. Oxford: Blackwell.

Welsh Office (1998) *Guidance on Early Years Education*. Cardiff: Welsh Office. (see website http://www.wales.gov.uk/)

Whitebread, D. (ed.) (1996) *Teaching and Learning in the Early Years*. London: Routledge.

Whitehead, M. (1999) *Support Language and Literacy Development in the Early Years*. Buckingham: Open University Press.

Wood, D. (1998) *How Children Think and Learn*, 2nd edn. Oxford: Blackwell.

Wood, L. and Attfield, J. (1996) *Play, Learning and the Early Childhood Curriculum*. London: Paul Chapman.

REFERENCES

CHILDREN'S BOOKS

Binns-McDonald, K. (1999) *Space Adventure*. Sydney, NSW: The Book Company.

Mayh, K. and Weir, D. (1993) *Knickerless Nicola*. London: Macmillan Children's Books.

Rosato, A. and Storey, R. (1992) *Goldilocks and Three Bears*. London: Viking.

ANNOTATED BIBLIOGRAPHY: EARLY YEARS TEXTS

There is a wide variety of early years texts and more are being published all the time. It is difficult to know what to include and what to omit and you will undoubtedly have your favourites. There are, inevitably, good texts we have not included. Note that the Pre-School Learning Alliance, Malling House, 45–49 Union Road, Croydon CR0 2XU has an excellent list of publications, ranging from practical booklets to more 'academic' texts.

ASSESSMENT, PLANNING AND OBSERVATION

Bartholomew, L. and Bruce, T. (1999) *Getting to Know You: A Guide to Record-keeping in Early Childhood Education and Care*, 2nd edn. London: Hodder & Stoughton.
Children learn through and with the people they love and the people who care for them; they learn through being physically active and through real direct experiences. This updated text builds on these precepts. It is a user-friendly book and while it incorporates the latest research on early childhood education, it also provides plenty of practical help.

Blenkin, G.M. and Kelly, A.V. (eds) (1991) *Assessment in Early Childhood Education*. London: Paul Chapman.
A good discussion of the merits of both formative and summative assessment and the conflict that can arise between the two approaches. Chapter 7 by Eve Gregory and Clare Kelly is good on 'Bilingualism and Assessment'.

Drummond, M.J., Rouse, D. and Pugh, G. (1992) *Making Assessment Work*. London: Arnold/National Children's Bureau.
This text highlights the importance of observation. It is 'all too easy to make judgements based on assumptions . . . not on what children actually do'. The authors remind us that we need to be aware of what our assumptions are – and then check whether they are right by observing the child in action.

Harding, J. and Meldon-Smith, L. (1996) *How to Make Observations and Assessments*. London: Hodder & Stoughton.
Jackie Harding and Liz Meldon-Smith tackle the issue by providing practical guidance with the key skills of observing and interpreting children's behaviour. The authors state their aims clearly and each chapter starts with its own specific objectives, which provide a guide for readers.

Hutchin, V. (1996) *Tracking Significant Achievement in the Early Years*. London: Hodder & Stoughton.
To write this book Vicky Hutchin examined over 100 samples of 'significant achievement' for children between the ages of 3 and 6 years. Almost every one of these involved some kind of change or development in attitude, such as confidence, persistence or independence. Reading this will help you convince other professionals that attitudes to learning and towards self are very important for this age group.

Hutchin, V. (1999) *Right from the Start: Effective Planning and Assessment in the Early Years*. London: Hodder & Stoughton.
A very readable and wide-ranging text on planning, assessment and record-keeping. The author gives practical advice with ideas that really work. The examples of good practice are drawn from real settings and illustrated with children's drawings and talk. The author includes details on how planning is affected by the teaching strategies staff use and the way in which the learning environment is organized.

Rodger, R. (1999) *Planning an Appropriate Curriculum for the Under Fives*. London: David Fulton.
This text is a great help for different types of planning in

all six areas of the 'Early Learning Goals'. There are practical points, such as a useful list of questions to help evaluate your half-term programme (p. 35).

Sayeed, Z. and Guerin, E. (2000) *Early Years Play: A Happy Medium for Assessment and Intervention*. London: David Fulton.
Provides a description and analysis of play and its use in helping young children to reach their potential. It is particularly useful for professionals working with young children with special educational needs and from a range of cultural and linguistic backgrounds. It is also aimed at parents and carers.

CHILD DEVELOPMENT

Bee, H. (1997) *The Developing Child*, 8th edn. London: Harper Collins
This very detailed book guides you through some quite complicated material, but always demonstrates the relevance of the material to everyday life. There are many fascinating bits of information, such as the photographic evidence (in the section on perceptual development) of newborn babies' facial responses to different tastes.

Bredekamp, S. (ed.) (1987) *Developmentally Appropriate Practice in Early Childhood Programs Serving Children from Birth Through Age 8*. Washington, DC: National Association for the Education of Young Children.
Provides guidelines to help teachers, parents, administrators and policy-makers make informed decisions about the education of young children. The editor pleads for a thorough understanding of 'typical child development' and emphasizes that 'primary age children need to be active' (p. 63).

Brigid, D., Wasser, S. and Gilligan, R. (1999) *Child Development for Child Care and Protection Workers*. London: Jessica Kingsley.
This is the first study of child development to be written for practitioners in the child care and protection field, but it is relevant to us all. It summarizes important current thinking on child development and applies it to practice. It has an extensive bibliography to extend your reading.

Bryant, B. and Bradley, L. (1985) *Children's Reading Problems*. Oxford: Blackwell.
The authors show how significant experience and knowledge of rhyme and patterns in language are for children's development.

Harding, J. and Meldon-Smith, L. (1996) *Helping Young Children to Develop*. London: Hodder & Stoughton.
Simple, straightforward but detailed guide to child development up to 7 years and covers children with special educational needs up to 8 years. The authors emphasize the different needs of children and include ideas for activities. Their descriptions of children's development at different ages is sensibly titled 'Approaching Three Years and Over', etc. There is also an informed section on 'Observing children, record keeping and taking action'.

Isaacs, S. (1929) *The Nursery Years: The Mind of the Child from Birth to Six Years*. London: Routledge & Kegan Paul.
There are many 'old' texts which we could have included. This is a seminal one. Despite being written nearly 80 years ago, this is still a good, accessible read. Chapter 1 starts with 'What Should We Do?' and Chapter 8's discussion of 'Playthings' is so timely in our overly plastic world.

Nutbrown, C. (1999) *Threads of Thinking*, 2nd edn. London: Paul Chapman.
There are some excellent sections on the development of literacy, scientific and mathematical learning in Part Three. The author includes practical ideas for developing these concepts in young children. This book abounds with valuable ideas and suggestions that are grounded in a sound knowledge of child development.

Sheridan, M. (1997) *From Birth to Five Years*, 4th revised edn. Windsor: NFER-Nelson.
A stalwart standby for early years practitioners. It's a quick *aide-mémoire* for experienced practitioners. If you have a new colleague who has missed out on this or has only worked with older children, then give him or her this as bedtime reading.

Smith, P.K., Cowie, H. and Blades, M. (1998) *Understanding Children's Development*, 3rd edn. Oxford: Blackwell.
Difficult concepts are addressed with many clear examples. The bulk of the book deals with 'The social world of the child' and 'Children's developing minds'. Turn to page 316 for the table showing 'Stages in the development of question forms', which gives details of Adam's development from 28 to 42 months, and you will see the approach typical of this text.

Vygotsky, L. (1999) *Thought and Language*. Cambridge, MA: MIT Press
A newly revised and edited edition by Alex Kozulin, which contains new material and many references that were previously unavailable. Worth dipping into to deepen your thinking on the development of children's speech, thought and concepts. Do read the section which deals with 'the flaws in Piaget's theory'.

Wells, G. (1986) *The Meaning Makers: Children Learning Language and Using Language to Learn*. London: Hodder & Stoughton.
This is based on the Bristol study 'Language at Home and at School', which the author directed. It deals with

children's language and follows the development of a representative sample of children from their first words to the end of primary education. It reminds us that children play an active role in their own learning. This research also shows us how children operate at much higher levels of understanding and with greater skill if what we are trying to show and teach them is *meaningful* to them. It also shows how important children's experiences are in creating their own stories in play to the process of learning to read.

EARLY YEARS CURRICULUM ISSUES

Anning, A. (ed.) (1995) *A National Curriculum for the Early Years*. Buckingham: Open University Press.
This will help your thinking on the suitable content of an early years curriculum. If you only read one chapter, make it Chapter 12: 'The way ahead: Another National Curriculum for Key Stage One?' The editor's philosophy is summed up in her dedication: 'For all the Key Stage One teachers who struggled to manage the unmanageable'.

DES (1990) *Starting with Quality*. Report of the Rumbold Committee of Inquiry. London: DES.
Worth reading to remind experienced, and to tell newly qualified, practitioners that young children do not just respond to what we plan to teach: 'Children are affected by the contexts in which learning takes place, the people involved in it, and the values and beliefs which are embedded in it. The process of education – how children are encouraged to learn – is as important as, and inseparable from the content – what they learn'.

Drury, R., Miller, L. and Campbell, R. (2000) *Looking at Early Years Education and Care*. London: David Fulton.
The contributors' wide range of backgrounds in health and education ensures that a variety of issues are successfully covered. This book deals with health issues; bilingualism; special educational needs; the early years curriculum; the role of adults and parents working with young children's learning. The authors also bear in mind the demands of the National Literacy and Numeracy Strategies and set their discussions in the framework of the Foundation Stage.

Edwards, A. and Knight, P. (1994) *Effective Early Years Education*. Buckingham: Open University Press.
Concise and accessible. It will develop your thinking, and hopefully your practice, on exactly *what* we are teaching young children and *why*. Useful bullet points. The authors have taught and it shows. Chapter 3 on play is worth reading.

Fisher, J. (1998) *Starting with the Child*. Buckingham: Open University Press.
The author concerns herself with the question, 'Is the notion of a curriculum centred on the needs and interests of children more rhetoric than reality?' She examines how to keep a balance between the demands of the curriculum and the learning needs of the child. Make sure you read Chapter 7: 'The place of play: The status of child-initiated experiences'. Julie Fisher covers a wide range of topics and, like many of our texts, could be included in other categories (e.g. she has a concise section on planning).

Robson, S. and Smedley, S. (eds) (1996) *Education in Early Childhood: First Things First*. London: David Fulton.
The chapters address several important early years issues. Sue Robson stresses the importance of appraising and organizing the physical environment. Pat Gura's chapter on 'An entitlement curriculum for early childhood' reminds us of young children's educational rights and needs.

Smidt, S. (1998) *A Guide to Early Years Practice*. London: Routledge.
Eminently readable and knowledgeable. The author addresses the question of 'What should we do to promote children's learning in the early years?' There is an abundance of sound ideas that will help you deliver the best curriculum and promote the children's learning. As the author writes when discussing observation, 'It is time consuming and difficult, but worth the effort' (p. 125).

Whitebread, D. (ed.) (1996) *Teaching and Learning in the Early Years*. London: Routledge.
This book provides a review of best practice within nursery and infant education and is based on the standpoint that an effective early years curriculum must start with the children and their needs. All 18 chapters are enthusiastically written. Boxes at the end of chapters summarize their key elements and present a thorough overview of early years pedagogy.

PLAY

Several of the texts in this bibliography make important observations on play (see, for example, Edwards and Knight 1994; Sayeed and Guerin 2000).

Klugman, E. and Smilansky, S. (eds) (1990) *Children's Play and Learning*. New York/London: Teachers' College Press.
Chapter 2 is worth looking at for Sara Smilansky's research and findings on 'Sociodramatic play: Its relevance to behavior [sic] and achievement in school' (pp. 18–42). She provides evidence for the significance of 'dramatic and sociodramatic play' and reminds us how important it is to include this for children to develop and learn successfully.

Matterson, E. (1987) *Play with a Purpose for Under Sevens.* Harmondsworth: Penguin.
Chapters 1–4 are very accessible and useful for reminding us all of what young children need – at least sometime, somehow in the day. She deals with not just the types of activity but the variety of resources that will aid their development and learning.

Moyles, J. (ed.) (1994) *The Excellence of Play.* Buckingham: Open University Press.
Several early years experts cum practitioners combine to produce a book that addresses a variety of important areas. It argues that we need 'a curriculum which sanctions and utilises play [which] is more likely to provide well-balanced citizens of the future as well as happier children in the present'. Some of the texts this book holds dear are:

> 'Deep involvement by children is necessary and must be allowed and encouraged by the adults if the play is to be really challenging and contribute fully to the learning process', (Moyles, p. 9).

> 'play is, and should be, the right of every child' (Curtis, p. 36). She gives a perspective from her wide experience of play in different cultures.

The pedagogy of this book, and several in this bibliography, is summed up by Anning on p. 75, when she quotes Newton's *Ascent of Man*:

> 'I do not know what I may appear to the world, but to myself I seem to have been only like a boy playing on the sea shore diverting himself and then finding a smoother pebble or a prettier shell than ordinary while the greater ocean of truth lay all un-discovered before me'.

She then concludes Chapter 5 with: 'It would be a real achievement to educate young children who became adults with such a sense of curiosity and playfulness'. Make sure you read the 'Conclusion' at the end of every chapter.

Nutbrown, C. (ed.) (1996) *Children's Rights and Early Education.* London: Paul Chapman.
Read Tricia David's chapter on 'Their right to play'. It may help you update your early years policy and persuade colleagues, heads and governors of the contribution that play makes to a successful education.

Sheridan, M. (1999) Revised and updated by Harding, J. and Meldon-Smith, L. *Play in Early Childhood: From Birth to Six Years.* London: Routledge.
This second edition has been thoroughly revised and updated to meet the needs of a variety of early years workers. It has over 80 illustrations and descriptions of play at each stage of development from birth to 6 years. At the back is a useful list of organizations that support play.

Singer, D. and Singer, J. (1990) *The House of Make-Believe.* London: Harvard University Press.
A challenging read, but Chapter 7 on 'Creating an environment for imaginative play' has some very good points and will make you assess your provision.

Wood, E. and Attfield, J. (1996) *Play, Learning and the Early Childhood Curriculum.* London: Paul Chapman.
This book provides a detailed exploration of play, its relationship to learning and how it can be integrated into the early childhood curriculum. The authors suggest practical strategies for improving the quality of play. There are ideas for structuring play environments and developing the practitioner's role. Chapter 7 is particularly good on assessment.

PRACTICAL ASPECTS OF WORKING IN EARLY YEARS

Anning, A. and Edwards, A. (1999) *Promoting Children's Learning from Birth to Five.* Buckingham: Open University Press.
The complexity of addressing the various cognitive, social, physical and emotional learning needs of young children is discussed. The authors explore practical strategies to develop children's learning. This book will reassure early childhood practitioners and should also be mandatory reading for some heads and governors.

Caddell, D. (1998) *Numeracy in the Early Years: What the Research Tells us. Early Education Support.* Dundee: Scottish Consultative Council on the Curriculum.
Written to encourage educators in the early years to reflect on their current practice in teaching young children. It has many practical examples of how to work with young children to develop their numeracy skills. It also has a brief, but clear, section on 'Play as a context for early mathematical experiences'.

Cook, D. and Finlayson, H. (1999) *Interactive Children: Communicative Teaching. ICT and Classroom Teaching.* Buckingham: Open University Press.
Gives detailed information on how to provide rich learning experiences for children through the use of ICT. If you are uncertain about the opportunities that ICT offers, this gives a lot of practical guidance. Figure 1.2 (p. 18) emphasizes that ICT should not be just computers; it details all the aspects of 'electronic applications' that we should ensure children experience.

Drummond, M.J. and Pollard, A. (eds) (1997) *One Child, Many Worlds.* London: David Fulton.
By drawing on the experiences of children aged 3–8 years attending schools in Britain, Germany, Iceland, Australia and the USA, the authors of 11 case studies provide

insights into what it means for young children to enter a new language and culture in school. The five principles and associated questions (on pp. 4–6) that are developed by each contributor will help in your setting's multicultural thinking.

Drummond, M.J., Lally, M. and Pugh, G. (1989) *Working with Children: Developing a Curriculum for the Early Years*. Nottingham: NES/NCB.
A learning pack to support early years workers in nurseries, schools, playgroups, day nurseries and family centres. It will help you examine your current practice and is particularly good on observing children, looking at your role and the values that underpin your work. Their definition of 'curriculum' is one of the best we have come across.

Duffy, B. (1998) *Supporting Creativity and Imagination in the Early Years*. Buckingham: Open University Press.
This book is awash with 'how to do it' bullet points, tables, explanations illustrated by real examples from children's work. Each chapter begins with 'This chapter will look at . . .' and finishes with 'Summary', 'Further reading' and 'Things to think about'. The author's approach is summed up by her quotation of Keats: 'I am certain of nothing but the holiness of the heart's affections and the truth of imagination'.

Fisher, R. (1995) *Teaching Children to Learn*. Cheltenham: Stanley Thornes.
Covers several important areas. Make sure you read the paragraph on p. 152 dealing with what a 'powerful learning environment' provides.

Gura, P. (1996) *Resources for Early Learning: Children, Adults and Stuff*. London: Hodder & Stoughton.
Different types of stuff, such as beads, blocks, climbing frames and 'found materials', are used to explore and illustrate the vital role of people in seeing the possibilities of materials as crucial tools for children's successful all-round development.

Kenner, C. (2000) *Literacy Links for Bilingual Children*. Stoke-on-Trent: Trentham Books.
Practical guidance on creating a multilingual literary environment in early years settings. The author draws on research in a south London nursery class with case studies showing how practitioners can build on home literacy experiences to stimulate children's writing.

Moyles, J. (1992) *Organizing for Learning in the Primary Classroom*. Buckingham: Open University Press.
Explores the issues of *why* teachers do *what* they do, and is another text that is useful for all early years practitioners. Chapter 7 is typical of the author's attention to detail with its checklists and bullet points to help you evaluate classroom organization and management of the physical spaces in your setting.

Moyles, J. (ed.) (1995) *Beginning Teaching: Beginning Learning*. Buckingham: Open University Press.
Aimed at beginning primary teachers with the wish to help them survive and enjoy their chosen career. There are many good chapters relevant to all early years practitioners, particularly Roger Merry (Chapter 5) on children needing to learn learning strategies.

Roffey, S. (1999) *Special Needs in the Early Years*. London: David Fulton.
Good communication between parents, early years practitioners and other professionals is vital in ensuring continuity of progress for all children, but particularly for those with special educational needs. This book aims to save time and ensure that children's needs are met by gathering together information from a variety of contexts.

Roffey, S. and O'Reirdan, J. (1998) *Infant Classroom Behaviour, Needs, Perspectives and Strategies*. London: David Fulton.
The authors have used their own experiences, good practice and research to find answers to the perennial and growing problem of 'How can staff minimize disruptive and difficult behaviour?' Packed with sensible, workable ideas – the symbol of a hand pointer is used in the text to indicate practical strategies.

Smidt, S. (ed.) (1998) *The Early Years: A Reader*. London: Routledge.
This reader contains a series of specially commissioned articles that are written in a range of styles and voices. A fascinating read that includes children's and students' voices. The introduction by Lilian Katz on 'What is basic for young children' sets the tone, which is one of respect for children.

Wolfendale, S. (ed.) (2000) *Special Needs in the Early Years: Snapshots of Practice*. London: Routledge.
The snapshots of practice referred to in the title encapsulate a wealth of useful information and ideas, such as the useful addresses list on p. 44. The editor's intention was to answer the question, 'What is good and innovative practice when teaching early years children with special needs?'

PRACTITIONERS REFLECTING ON PRACTICE

Anning, A. (1997) *The First Years at School*, 2nd edn. Buckingham: Open University Press.
The author has worked alongside and talked with primary teachers for 20 years. This book reflects her experiences and shows a broad and detailed knowledge of research and practice. As Ted Wragg wrote of the first edition: 'I found the whole account a model of clarity with a good

blend of theory and practice which many authors would do well to note'.

David, T. (ed.) (1999) *Teaching Young Children*. London: Sage/Paul Chapman.
Tricia David starts the book with a commitment to the importance of relationships. The impact of emotional aspects of a school or nursery has been neglected in the UK, and the contributors to this book all recognize the need to develop this side of a child for successful education. The book discusses 'what childhood is for and what education is for'.

Early Childhood Education Forum (1998) *Quality in Diversity in Early Learning*. London: National Children's Bureau.
The ECEF is a consortium of the major national organizations concerned with the care and education of young children. This framework was produced by the collaboration of a very considerable number of early childhood professionals and aims to enable early childhood practitioners to think about, understand, support and extend the learning of young children from birth to age 8. One of the central principles is that 'young children are to be valued'. Section Three on 'Learning, play and children's entitlements' is essential reading.

Edgington, M. (1998) *The Nursery Teacher in Action: Teaching 3, 4 and 5 Year Olds*. London: Paul Chapman.
Written by the former Margaret Lally, this book explores in depth the work of the nursery teacher. It takes as its premise: 'The teaching of young children has long been undervalued and misunderstood – those who do it well find their role hard to explain because it involves such a wide range of complex responsibilities'. It is also a perfect example of how difficult it is to categorize these texts (e.g. Chapter 5 deals very well with 'Keeping records: Planning and assessment').

George, D. (1995) *The Challenge of the Able Child*, 2nd edn. London: David Fulton.
Although this book is aimed primarily at primary and secondary teachers and deals solely with the National Curriculum, some of the author's concerns echo ours in StEPs' *Too Busy to Play*. Chapter 6 addresses 'The parent/ child/teacher model' and has a section called 'Look at the whole child'. The quotation at the start of this chapter will give you a flavour: 'After you understand about the sun and the stars and the rotation of the earth, you may **still** miss the radiance of the sunset' (A.N. Whitehead).

Goleman, D. (1996) *Emotional Intelligence: Why it can Matter more than IQ*. London: Bloomsbury.
Only in recent years has there emerged a scientific model of the emotional mind. Daniel Goleman, writing from an American perspective in this meaty text, argues that our view of human intelligence is far too narrow. Emotional intelligence includes self-awareness, impulse control, persistence and empathy, all qualities that early years practitioners develop in young children.

Merry, R. (1998) *Successful Children: Successful Teaching*. Buckingham: Open University Press.
Although this book is aimed at primary teachers, it is worth a look at if only you read the section on providing a 'comfortable challenge' (pp. 116–27). The book deals with

- What do we now know about how children learn.
- How can teachers come to understand the processes of successful teaching better.
- How can we apply an improved understanding of successful teaching and learning, given the constraints of the primary context.

Rodd, J. (1999) *Leadership in Early Childhood: The Pathway to Professionalism*, 2nd edn. Buckingham: Open University Press.
A sentence from the editor's acknowledgements best sums up this book: 'The product of over twenty years experience in the early childhood field and is a reflection of my opportunities to meet and work with many of the gifted and dedicated women and the few men who make up the field, including family day-care providers and coordinators, child-care workers, pre-school teachers and directors, government administrators and academic educators'.

Siraj-Blatchford, I. and Clarke, P. (2000) *Supporting Identity, Diversity and Language in the Early Years*. Buckingham: Open University Press.
This book is part of a series called 'Supporting early learning'. All the texts subscribe to a set of nine principles for a developmental curriculum and aim to help you evaluate ideas about the most effective ways of educating young children. This book provides clear evidence and practical guidance on how to work with young children in developing a positive disposition towards themselves regardless of their differences.

Smith, A. and Langston, A. (1999) *Managing Staff in Early Years Settings*. London: Routledge.
Although this book deals with management theory, don't let this put you off. It has interesting case studies and useful 'Reflection' boxes, which will aid your thinking on your own setting. If you are having a stressful day, don't do the 'A/B Lifestyle Questionnaire' on pp. 176–8. If you want a boost, read the last page first.

Smith, E.A. (1994) *Educating the Under Fives*. London: Cassell.
This is interesting if you want to put early years into the historical context of the last 30–40 years. It also has an informed section on 'The range of provision' with a useful bibliography.

TOPIC INDEX

accountablity, 2
adult role, 3, 14, 10, 20, 27, 31, 33, 35, 36, 39, 40, 43, 46, 49, 51, 61, 64, 67, 70, 74, 78, 79, 84, 86, 90, 91
articulation, 2, 4, 9
assessment, 8, 35, 61

baseline assessment, 21, 60, 61, 64

child development, 4, 7, 8, 9, 25, 33, 39, 41, 43, 46, 49, 51, 58, 59, 61, 62, 87, 90, 91
citizenship, 60, 66
creative development, 32, 80
culture, 5, 26, 59, 63, 69
curriculum, 6, 7

development
  creative, 32, 80
  emotional, 8, 9, 26, 31, 41, 43, 46, 49, 52, 54, 62, 67, 76, 87, 92
  intellectual, 8, 20, 35, 40, 43, 46, 49, 51, 54, 67, 76, 78, 85, 87
  linguistic, 24, 25, 30, 41, 47, 50, 51, 68, 76, 78, 85, 87
disability, 5

emotional development, 8, 9, 26, 31, 41, 43, 46, 49, 52, 54, 62, 67, 76, 87, 92
entitlement, 4, 24
equality, 4, 5
ethnicity, 5, 26, 63
evaluation, 34

faith, 5, 26, 63
Foundation Stage, 2, 58, 59, 81

gender, 5

intellectual development, 8, 20, 35, 40, 43, 46, 49, 51, 54, 67, 76, 78, 85, 87

knowledge and understanding of the world, 24, 26, 87

language, 8, 20, 26, 27, 31, 60, 61, 80, 94
learning environment, 83
life-long learning, 2
linguistic development, 24, 25, 30, 41, 47, 50, 51, 68, 76, 78, 85, 87
literacy, 6, 20, 25, 26, 31, 70, 79, 74

meaningful and relevant activities and contexts, 63–4, 68

numeracy, 6, 20, 24, 31, 33, 34, 60, 61, 70

observation, 8, 23, 38, 60, 61, 71
outdoor play, 80

parents, 21, 64
pedagogical knowledge, 4, 7
physical development, 6, 8, 20, 32, 40, 41, 45, 48, 51, 53, 62, 65, 67, 78, 85, 91
planning, 3, 5, 6, 7, 9, 21, 25, 27, 28, 31, 34, 35, 62, 75
play, 2, 3, 4, 8, 9, 10, 11, 14, 20, 26, 27, 30, 33, 35, 59, 60, 62, 63, 65, 70, 71, 76
principles, 4
problem solving, 65
progression, 8
provision, 5, 6, 7, 8, 33, 69, 86

recording, 8
reflective practice, 11, 21, 38, 81

respect, 4, 7
rights, 2

safety, 9
scaffolding, 66

social development, 8, 9, 24, 25, 26, 27, 30, 39, 41, 45, 48, 51, 55, 60, 61, 62, 63, 67, 71, 76, 85, 87, 90
society, 2, 7
special educational needs, 5
spiritual development, 59

AUTHOR INDEX

Adams, S., 2
Anning, A. and Edwards, A., 68
Athey, C., 33

Barnardos, 68
Bennett, N. *et al.*, 9
Beetlestone, F., 65
Bilton, H., 62
Binns-McDonald, 25
Birmingham City Council/NFER-Nelson, 60
Blakemore, C., 9
Bredekamp, S., 64
Bruce, T., 10

Claxton, G., 68
Cook, H. and Finlayson, H., 68
Curtis, A., 6

de Boo, M., 65
DfEE, 20, 59, 60
Donaldson, M., 64
Duffy, B., 64, 66, 98

Edwards, A. and Knight, P., 68
Elkind, D., 69
Early Childhood Education Forum/National Children's Bureau (ECEF/NCB), 7, 20
Early Years Curriculum Group (EYCG), 20

Fisher, J., 63, 67

Galton, M. *et al.*, 67
Goleman, D., 8, 70

Healy, J., 68
Hurst, V. and Joseph, J., 8
Hutchin, V., 71

Katz, L., 9
Kotulak, R., 74
Kozulin, 66

Lindon, J., 66

Maude, P., 65
Merry, M., 8, 63
Moriarty, V. and Siraj-Blatchford, I., 7
Moyles, J., 7, 64, 66, 71, 94
Moyles, J. and Suschitzky, W., 6

NFER, 60
Norway Royal Ministry of Church, Education and Research, 58
Nutbrown, C., 20

OHMCI, 58

Pascal, C. and Bertram, A., 63
Parliamentary Office of Science and Technology (POST), 74

QCA/DfEE, 58, 59
Qualifications and Curriculum Authority (QCA), 4, 58, 60

Roberts, R., 7, 62
Robinson, K., 20

Scottish Education Department (SED), 58
Siraj-Blatchford, I., 7, 62

Siraj-Blatchford, I. and Clarke, P., 62
Smilansky, S., 10
Smilansky, S. and Shefatya, L., 10
Sutton-Smith, B., 9

Vygotsky, L., 66

Webb, L., 7
Welsh Office, 58
Whitebread, D., 7
Whitehead, M., 63
Wood, D., 71
Wood, L. and Attfield, J., 9, 96